JOURNEY
TO A BETTER PLACE

JOURNEY

TO A BETTER PLACE

A WOMEN'S GUIDED STUDY OF HEBREWS

CYNTHIA DIANNE GUY

Gospel Advocate
Nashville, Tennessee

Also by Cynthia Dianne Guy

What About the Women?

Struggle Seek Grow

Published by Gospel Advocate Co.
1006 Elm Hill Pike, Nashville, TN 37210
www.gospeladvocate.com

ISBN 10: 0-89225-669-9

ISBN 13: 978-0-89225-669-3

This book is dedicated to my Christian sisters

in the Myrtle Beach Church of Christ

for their love, encouragement, and helpful comments

in the writing of this study guide.

I also dedicate this work to

my godly grandmother, Julia Redden,

who celebrates her 100th birthday in 2017,

the year of this book's publication.

CONTENTS

Introduction: Letter of Encouragement.............................ix

Chapter 1: Follow God's Son 1

Chapter 2: Don't Drift from the Path 9

Chapter 3: Persevere to the End............................. 21

Chapter 4: Look for a Good Rest Stop................................31

Chapter 5: Are We There Yet? 41

Chapter 6: Keep Moving Forward 53

Chapter 7: Follow the Guide 65

Chapter 8: Turn Right at the Fork............................ 77

Chapter 9: Ask for Directions................................. 91

Chapter 10: Walk with One Another 105

Chapter 11: Visit the Landmarks 119

Chapter 12: Heaven Is the Better Place 131

Chapter 13: Postscripts..143

Notes 153

LETTER OF ENCOURAGEMENT

The movie *Love Comes Softly* opens with a young pioneer woman traveling northwest with her husband to begin a new life. They had drifted from the trail and were weary. Obstacles and disappointments had blinded Marty to the reason for her journey. She vented her frustration: "I'm tired, sick and tired of this dirt and miles that seem to lead nowhere and the layers of dust on my skin." This was vastly different from her anticipation at the beginning, when she said, "I was always positive about my hopes and dreams. My eyes were always on the end of the trail." The hazards of the journey had discouraged Marty, and she was tempted to turn back to her comfortable, old life. Happily, in time, she regained her perspective, accepted encouragement from others, and achieved her dream.

A similar narrative is beautifully presented in the book of Hebrews. When we begin the Christian life, we set out on a journey to a better place. We will face obstacles and disappointments. We will be tempted to turn back to comfortable, old ways. But the encouragement of our brothers and sisters and a focus on heaven will help us remain on the trail and achieve our dream of heaven.

Imagine being Marty's mother, best friend, or older mentor. You know she needs your encouragement. You want to help. Phones and computers are yet to be invented, and you are too far away to put your arms around her. How can you help? You sit down with pen and paper and do what people did for centuries to lift up loved ones who were far away—you write a letter of encouragement.

Hebrews is such a letter. It was written to first-century Hebrew Christians who were struggling, discouraged, and considering going back to their old Jewish faith. Judaism was on the list of legal religions in the Roman Empire, but Christianity was not. These converts were beginning to feel the heat of persecution, and they were not strong enough spiritually to cope. Their journey toward heaven was strewn with disappointments, which left them weary. They felt sick and tired of emotional miles that seemed to lead nowhere. These frustrations blinded them to the reason for their journey.

This was vastly different from their anticipation at the beginning. Soon after their conversion, these Jewish Christians were spiritually strong. They stood against harassment for their new beliefs in a crucified Savior and for rituals like the weekly consumption of His body and blood. They were convinced this new faith had more to offer than the old. Neil Lightfoot reflected, "They had been exposed to public shame; they had joyfully accepted the plundering of their goods, knowing that they had 'a better possession and an abiding one' (10:33-34)."[1] They felt confident in their journey to a better place.

But over time, their strength waned. Christian mentors had died, and those left behind began to drift away from the faith. They neglected study of God's word and regular worship and, thus, failed to grow spiritually. Without maturity-producing Scripture and encouragement from Christian brothers and sisters, they became "weary and discouraged" (Hebrews 12:3) and vulnerable to "various and strange doctrines" (13:9).[2]

Spiritually, they suffered from "hands which hang down" and "feeble knees" (12:12). They were unprepared to face mounting persecution and were in danger of leaving Christianity (3:12). Many were tempted to turn back to their comfortable, old Jewish faith. The letter of Hebrews was written to encourage these Jewish converts to keep on keeping on in their Christian walk.

BACKGROUND OF THE LETTER

KEY WORD AND MESSAGE

The key word in Hebrews is the Greek term *kreitton*, meaning "better."[3] It occurs thirteen times in this letter. The general message is that Christianity is better than their former religion. Jesus Christ is better than the great Jewish leaders Abraham, Moses, Aaron, and Joshua. He is superior to the angels. He offers a better priesthood, sacrifice, and covenant than the Law of Moses. The blood of bulls and goats could not take away sin, but Christ's blood does. Therefore, the writer warned that to reject Christianity and turn back to Judaism would be spiritual suicide.

Before studying any Bible book, it is best to answer three questions:
1. Who wrote it?
2. To whom was it written?
3. What is the purpose of the writing?

AUTHOR OF THE LETTER

When you get a letter, what is the first thing you look for? The name of the sender! Some twenty of the twenty-one New Testament epistles open with the author's name. Romans begins, "Paul, a bondservant of Jesus Christ ... to all who are in Rome" (Romans 1:1, 7). The first verses of James and Jude read, respectively, "James, a bondservant of God and of the Lord Jesus Christ" and "Jude, a bondservant of Jesus Christ." But Hebrews has no salutation. Its anonymity is one of the great mysteries of the New Testament.

Some believe the thoughts sound like Paul, but not the style and composition. Paul knew Hebrew; but this writer quoted from the Septuagint (the Greek translation of the Hebrew Old Testament). Some suggest the letter was written by Barnabas, Luke, Clement of Rome, or Apollos.[4] One third-century church father, Origen, concluded that "God only knows the truth."[5] The letter shows that the author had a relationship with his readers. He knew about their early spiritual fervor, cared enough to urge them to persevere, and expected to visit them again (Hebrews 10:32; 13:19).

Hebrews is unique in other ways too. Some suggest it was written to a small, weak faction in one congregation because of its warnings and greetings to "all those who rule over you, and all the saints" (Hebrews 13:24).[6] Another interesting proposal is that this was a sermon. The original writer described it as "the word of exhortation" (v. 22). James Thompson suggested its style and method of argument are like a sermon in the ancient synagogue and the ending salutation could be from one who wrote down the sermon and sent it to friends.[7] Have you ever requested a copy of a sermon to send to loved ones? Perhaps an eloquent writer copied this one and sent it to struggling Jewish converts. As an inspired letter, Hebrews continues to encourage today.

RECIPIENTS OF THE LETTER

Early manuscripts titled the letter "To Hebrews." In the New Testament, this term refers to people who used the Hebrew language in public worship and kept Hebrew customs and traditions.[8] Recipients were ethnically Jewish, but spiritually Christian. They were well acquainted with Jewish concepts and Old Testament texts. The writer generously sprinkled these as illustrations and evidences throughout the letter.

Hebrews was written to a group of Jewish Christians in a specific place. Some believe they lived in Jerusalem.[9] Others say they were in Rome.[10] The time of the writing was probably between A.D. 64 and 69. Persecution under Roman emperor Nero took place during this time. R.C.H. Lenski described the recipients' spiritual condition:

> In this body of Jewish Christians a movement is under way to give up Christianity and to go back to their former Judaism. This movement has as yet not gained much momentum, no members have actually apostatized, the leaders still stand firm. This body of Jewish Christians has suffered some persecution for sympathizing with brethren who are of their own body but were imprisoned (10:32-34), yet none of the readers were themselves imprisoned at that time, and none of them had lost their lives by martyrdom (12:4). This entire body of Jewish Christians had remained true during the trying times of the past; but

something now occurred which led a number of them to think that it would be a great advantage to them to go back to their old Judaism. It is this incipient defection which calls forth this letter.[11]

We have no way of knowing the exact date of writing. The author did not mention the destruction of Jerusalem (A.D. 70), but did refer to the priests' daily ministering (Hebrews 8:4; 10:11). So we can conclude that the temple with its sacrificial system was still intact. However, its end was coming soon (Matthew 24:15-22). Martel Pace concluded, "Hebrews, if written some time during A.D. 63-67, was perfectly timed to prepare Jewish Christians for the loss of their temple and all that it represented."[12]

PURPOSE OF THE LETTER

We all enjoy getting cards of encouragement, but sometimes we need a loving nudge to get up and continue on our journey. *The Pulpit Commentary* reveals,

> And there seems to have been at that time a peculiar need for the note of warning to be loud and rousing. For it appears from passages in the Epistle that some, at least, of the Hebrew Christians had shown signs of retrogression rather than of advance; they had not only failed to make the progress they should have done in appreciation of the true meaning of the gospel,—they were even in danger of falling back from it to their old position.[13]

Readers needed reminding that Christianity is better than the Jewish religion they left. The Law of Moses had served its purpose. It was a "tutor" to bring people to Christ (Galatians 3:24) and "a shadow of the good things to come" (Hebrews 10:1). Its animal sacrifices were never able to wash away sin. They were merely symbolic of the true sacrifice, Jesus and His saving blood. When He died, His new will and testament came into effect. A new covenant was established through His church. God's plan of salvation was complete; therefore, the old Jewish system was no longer necessary.

God's children in this new age are called Christians. Sisters, ours is a better journey. The Hebrews readers had experienced this better way.

They had enjoyed love, joy, peace, forgiveness, help in this life, and hope for eternity in heaven. But, in time, discouragement, stagnation, and persecution put them in danger of drifting away.

Drifting and temptation to leave the faith can occur when one loses sight of the better place. Neglect of Bible study and of fellowship can lead to apathy. Secular activities and peer pressure can distract. An entire group can grow weary and spend Sundays going through the motions. Some have left the church after years of assembling with lethargic congregants, dutifully enduring shallow studies of the Word and wondering why neighbors are not attracted to their Christian religion. The Hebrews letter is a wake-up call.

Have you or has someone close to you been tempted to leave the Christian faith? Discuss circumstances that prompted these thoughts.

Hebrews proclaims: "Don't leave! Jesus Christ is the only way to heaven. Study the Word. Stay in the faith. Stand firm in your commitment, even in the face of opposition. Walk with us in our journey to a better place." Now, let us open this letter to first-century Christians and discover its important message for us today.

CHAPTER 1

FOLLOW GOD'S SON
(HEBREWS 1)

Discouraged. This describes some first-century Jewish Christians. The Christian walk was not as easy as they had hoped. They believed in God and knew His word, but needed reminding of His more recent communication through Jesus. To end doubts about their new faith, the Hebrews writer began his letter with the powerful opening statement of Hebrews 1:1-3..

Spokesman for the Better Way (Hebrews 1:1-3)
1 God, who at various times and in various ways spoke in time past to the fathers by the prophets, 2 has in these last days spoken to us by His Son, whom He has appointed heir of all things, through whom also He made the worlds; 3 who being the brightness of His glory and the express image of His person, and upholding all things by the word of His power, when He had by Himself purged our sins, sat down at the right hand of the Majesty on high.

What an opening! This letter proclaimed that God—who revealed His will in times past only in pieces "at various times and in various ways"—had presented His better, new covenant with a complete and final revelation (Jude 3). This last and better message came through a superior spokesman, God's Son.

The temporary Law of Moses had ended. Christ's New Testament ushered in the Christian age (cf. Acts 2:17). This concept was beautifully pictured in Mark 9:2-8. Jesus had taken Peter, James, and John onto the Mount of Transfiguration. Suddenly, Moses and Elijah appeared next to Him. As Peter suggested that the men worship all three, God took away the lawgiver and prophet and proclaimed of Jesus, "This is My beloved Son. Hear Him!" (v. 7). Hebrews exalts God's Son as "the author and finisher of our faith" (12:2). He is the only way to the better place (John 14:6).

Read this teachable moment in Mark 9:2-8 (also in Matthew 17:1-8).
What was God's message about Jesus compared to Moses and Elijah?

Hebrews 1 is a treatise on the superiority of God's Son, on whom the Christian religion is based. These weak Jewish Christians needed encouragement. This letter can also strengthen faith in Christians today. Note that the writer did not yet use the name "Jesus" or the title "Christ." He described Him here as God's Son. The purpose was to emphasize His deity. Review Hebrews 1:2-3 to discover six statements of evidence of the Son's superiority.

1. God's Son is the "heir of all things" (Hebrews 1:2b). His inheritance, as the natural right of sonship, included the entire universe (Psalm 2:7-8; Matthew 28:18).

2. God's Son made the worlds (Hebrews 1:2b; John 1:1-3; Colossians 1:15-17).

3. God's Son is "the brightness of [God's] glory and the express image of His person" (Hebrews 1:3). The Greek term for "image" (*charakter*) means "impression" or "reproduction" as a seal left on wax.[14] Jesus said, "He who has seen Me has seen the Father" (John 14:9). He radiates the light of God's glory (2 Corinthians 4:4-6).

4. God's Son upholds all things (Hebrews 1:3). He not only made the world; He holds everything together and keeps it running smoothly.

5. God's Son washed away our sins (Hebrews 1:3). To redeem us, He served as both priest and offering. Scripture describes Him as the superior High Priest and the sacrificial Lamb. He shed His

own blood as the once-for-all offering. Without it, there could be no forgiveness of sins (9:28).

6. God's Son "sat down at the right hand of the Majesty on high" (Hebrews 1:3). This quote from Psalm 110:1 is the key text used by the early church to prove Jesus' Messiahship. Even the Jewish scribes believed this prophecy referred to the Messiah (Mark 12:35-37). At God's right hand, His Son sits in a place of honor and dominion.

The Son of God is Creator, Sustainer, Redeemer, and Exalted One at God's right hand. Jewish readers who believed and obeyed the Lord in baptism needed to realize His superiority. Why should they have considered going back to an old system that ended at His cross (Colossians 2:14)? Jesus, with everything He offers, is better.

Why should these six statements
about God's Son be emphasized today?

Superior to Angels (Hebrews 1:4-14)

4 *... having become so much better than the angels, as He has by inheritance obtained a more excellent name than they.* **5** *For to which of the angels did He ever say: "You are My Son, today I have begotten You"? And again: "I will be to Him a Father, and He shall be to Me a Son"?* **6** *But when He again brings the firstborn into the world, He says: "Let all the angels of God worship Him."* **7** *And of the angels He says: "Who makes His angels spirits and His ministers a flame of fire."* **8** *But to the Son He says: "Your throne, O God, is forever and ever; a scepter of righteousness is the scepter of Your kingdom.* **9** *You have loved righteousness and hated lawlessness; therefore God, Your God, has anointed You with the oil of gladness more than Your companions."* **10** *And: "You, Lord, in the beginning laid the foundation of the earth, and the heavens are the work of Your hands.* **11** *They will perish, but You remain; and they will all grow old like a garment;* **12** *like a cloak You will fold them up, and they will be changed. But You are the same, and Your years will not fail."* **13** *But to which of the angels has He ever said: "Sit at My right hand, till I make Your enemies Your footstool"?* **14** *Are they not all ministering spirits sent forth to minister for those who will inherit salvation?*

Next, the writer explained that God's Son is better than the angels. In that day, some engaged in angel worship (Colossians 2:18). A doctrine existed that Jesus was not deity, but an angelic being. Lightfoot commented, "The temptation for the ancients was to overemphasize either His humanity or His divinity. Perhaps the readers of the Epistle, or at least some of them, avoided both extremes by associating Jesus with the angelic creation."[15] Therefore, the writer needed to emphasize the Son's position and His name as "more excellent" (Hebrews 1:4).[16] The rest of Hebrews 1 proves this fact.

Jewish readers knew the Old Testament prophecies about the Messiah. The Hebrews writer chose six to show that God's Son—and not an angel—fulfilled these prophecies. If you are familiar with the Old Testament, these verses will offer a deeper understanding. If not, you may find this entire letter a bit overwhelming. If it is a sermon, it was written to strengthen faith. Sisters, stay in this study. It is not an easy read. But if you keep in mind its purpose to encourage perseverance in Christianity, you will come away spiritually stronger. You will learn much about the Old Testament and its role in God's plan of salvation. You will better appreciate the New Testament and its blessings.

Let us now review the final verses of Hebrews 1, in which the writer quoted from seven Old Testament passages to show God's Son is better than the angels. Underline the key thought in each verse. Ask yourself how it provides proof of His superiority. Do you see the evidence getting stronger with each verse?

The term "begotten," here, was a metaphor for "the act of enthronement."

Hebrews 1:5a quotes from Psalm 2:7. This (with verse 6) was the first proclamation of God's decree to set up His kingdom. He said, "You are My Son, today I have begotten You." Jewish readers recognized this prophecy as (1) an announcement about David as Israel's king and (2) a reference to David's seed, the Messiah, who would reign over the future spiritual kingdom. The term "begotten," here, was a metaphor for "the act of enthronement."[17]

Just as God placed David on an earthly throne, He later established His Son's spiritual kingship. The phrase "and again" in verse 5 means another Old Testament quote will follow. The letter uses this phrase often.

Hebrews 1:5b quotes 2 Samuel 7:14. God spoke these words through Nathan the prophet when King David wanted to build a house (temple) for God. In 2 Samuel 7:1-14, God explained that He did not need an earthly house and that a spiritual house and kingdom would be established through David's descendants. He used the word "seed" (v. 12), which refers to Jesus (John 7:42; Luke 1:32). The Hebrews writer used the prophecy "I will be to Him a Father, and He shall be to Me a Son" to show special relationship between God and Christ. Although angels have been called sons of God (Job 1:6; 2:1; 38:7), the writer asked, "To which of the angels did He ever say [these words]?" The answer is none. No angel ever experienced the relationship or position held by God's Son.

Hebrews 1:6 quotes Deuteronomy 32:43. The Father introduced His Son to the world as "the firstborn" (Colossians 1:15)—a status of privilege and favor in Old Testament families—and He instructed, "Let all the angels of God worship Him" (Hebrews 1:6). God's Son is better than the angels. They worship Him. Can you imagine these readers hanging their heads in shame because they had forgotten how wonderful Christ their Savior was? Do we not sometimes need this reminder too? He is superior to even the angels!

Hebrews 1:7 quotes from Psalm 104:4. It describes angels as mere servants—like the natural elements of wind and fire—to be transformed and sent at God's will (cf. Psalm 103:20; 104:4). In contrast, God's Son has authority! Surely, readers had heard about Jesus' Sermon on the Mount, when "He taught ... as one having authority" (Matthew 7:29). His authority extended even over God's heavenly messengers.

Hebrews 1:8-9 restates the Father's direct reference to His Son as "God" and prescribes for Him an eternal reign (cf. Psalm 45:6-7). He is so pleased with the Son's love for righteousness and hatred of lawlessness that He makes the kingly anointment with "the oil of gladness [joy]," more than all His companions. These include all other celestial beings. God's Son is the superior Messiah and King prophesied in the Old Testament. Jewish readers were raised on messianic psalms, but needed reminding that the Messiah had come!

Hebrews 1:10-12 notes that the Father calls the Son "Lord" and witnesses His role as Creator. He contrasts the temporary nature of the heavens and earth with the Son's eternality (cf. Psalm 102:25-27). Readers lived in a time when people called Caesar "Lord." They needed reminding of Jesus' superiority. God's Son is eternal and above all His creation. His words and the elements of His new covenant are far better than the old Jewish law system.

Hebrews 1:13 refers again to Psalm 110:1. Here, the writer asked, "But to which of the angels has He ever said: 'Sit at My right hand, till I make Your enemies Your footstool'?" In the presence of God, angels stand (Luke 1:19; Revelation 8:2). At God's right hand, Jesus sits (Hebrews 1:3) and reigns (1 Peter 3:22). On the day of judgment, the Father will strip all power from all enemies and make them utterly subject to His Son (Matthew 22:41-46; Acts 2:34-35).

The Messiah, God's Son, holds all authority (Matthew 28:18). The angels do not. He was reigning at the time Hebrews was written. He continues to reign as we read the letter today. His reign will continue until the end of time when God will send Him again to take all the living and dead to face judgment. Each of us must ask ourselves if we are submitting to God's Son, Jesus Christ, or have we left His path, the only path that leads to the better place?

The last verse in Hebrews 1 raises an interesting question about angels. What is meant by "ministering spirits sent forth to minister for those who will inherit salvation" (v. 14)?

Ministering spirits. "Ministering," here, means "public worship." Isaiah 6:2-3 beautifully describes these spirits as worshiping God, crying

"Holy, Holy, Holy is the LORD of hosts; the whole earth is full of His glory." Revelation 5:11-12 pictures them worshiping God's Son, saying, "Worthy is the Lamb who was slain to receive power and riches and wisdom, and strength and honor and glory and blessing!" Angels worship their superiors: God and His Son.

Minister for those who will inherit salvation. Angels also serve Christians, who enjoy the present and future aspects of salvation. Have you ever wondered how angels minister to us? *The Pulpit Commentary* suggests they are sent on "errands of helpfulness to God's people on earth in their times of emergency."[18] The Old Testament gives examples of angels delivering Lot, Jacob, and Daniel. It presents angels giving instruction to Abraham, Joshua, and Gideon. The New Testament shows angelic help for Jesus in Gethsemane (Luke 22:41-44) and Peter in prison (Acts 12:6-11). Is there evidence outside of Scripture? Rufinus, an ancient church historian, wrote about a Christian martyr named Theodorus, who asserted that, during torture, he felt comfort and support from a spirit-like presence.[19] Many people have experienced help in times of crisis. This verse offers comfort, but its main purpose is to provide contrast between the worshiping, helping role of angels and the superior role of God's Son.

Why do you think the writer emphasized
the superiority of God's Son over the angels?
How might this information be helpful for Christians today?

SUMMARY AND LOOKING FORWARD TO THE NEXT CHAPTER

This letter was written to Jewish Christians in danger of leaving the faith and returning to Judaism. Because of neglected Bible study and fellowship, some became discouraged on their journey to the better place. They had lost sight of their Savior. The writer reminded them that the same God who inspired Old Testament messages had proclaimed a final and complete revelation through His Son. This Creator, Sustainer, and Redeemer sits at God's right hand and is worshiped by the angels. He is the eternal Messiah and King to which the Old Testament prophesied. Sisters, He is Lord!

Upcoming chapters remind readers that God's Son fulfilled the old Jewish law. His death annulled that covenant and established a new one. Only under this new will and testament is salvation possible. The writer of Hebrews was concerned for his readers' souls. He warned them not to reject God's Son, leave Christianity, or go back to Judaism. Hebrews 2 explains the consequences of neglecting this great salvation. Christians today who are tempted to leave the faith can also benefit from its message.

CHAPTER 2

DON'T DRIFT FROM THE PATH
(HEBREWS 2)

Journeys are easiest on clear, level, well-marked roads. Before machinery and asphalt, paths had to be manually prepared. Perhaps you saw the episode of *Little House on the Prairie* featuring this work. Charles Ingalls and Mr. Edwards took a job transporting nitroglycerin. While one drove the wagonload of explosives, the other walked ahead to remove rocks and fill in holes. This created a better path for their journey. Both men knew that to turn or drift from the prepared road was dangerous. We, too, must be careful in our travels, both physically and spiritually, lest we drift from the right path and end up somewhere other than our desired destination.

Hebrews 2 presents a spiritual application. First-century Jews who converted to Christianity were on a journey to a better place. God's Son came to earth to clear the path. Wearing the earthly name "Jesus," He experienced temptations, suffering, and death to help us reach our spiritual destination. But without Bible study and fellowship, readers began to wander from the path and considered leaving it altogether. In the first few verses of Hebrews 2, the writer warned against drifting from that better way.

Warning against Drifting Away (Hebrews 2:1-4)
1 Therefore we must give the more earnest heed to the things we have heard, lest we drift away. 2 For if the word spoken through angels proved steadfast, and every transgression and disobedience received a just reward, 3 how shall we escape if we neglect so great a salvation, which at the first began to be spoken by the Lord, and was confirmed to us by those who

heard Him, 4 God also bearing witness both with signs and wonders, with various miracles, and gifts of the Holy Spirit, according to His own will?

New Testament letters were not written with chapter and verse divisions. Some suggest that Hebrews 2:1-4 forms a nice conclusion to chapter 1. Read it, and see if you agree. The writer had just presented six evidences for the superiority of God's Son. After these doctrinal truths, he used the term "therefore" to prompt the right response.

Because God has spoken to us by His Son (Hebrews 1:2), *"therefore we must give the more earnest heed to the things we have heard, lest we drift away"* (2:1). The New Testament message of Jesus Christ is from God! Therefore, we must earnestly obey. These Christians had obeyed the gospel, but they were not diligent in following its teachings.

Define the term "diligent." Why is it important for Christians to be diligent when it comes to studying and following Scripture?

When we do not take Christianity seriously, when we miss worship and neglect Bible study, and when we are unconcerned about lost souls, we are off course in our spiritual journey. The Hebrews readers were in danger of drifting away from the faith.

We are familiar with the phrase "drift away." It is a subtle movement that can go unnoticed until it is too late. Sometimes it has tragic results. As mothers and sisters, we are touched by the following sad, but true, illustration:

> Two young men were fishing above a low dam on a river near their hometown. As they were concentrating on catching fish, they were unaware that they had drifted until they were not far from the water flowing over the dam. When they realized their situation, the current near the dam had become too powerful for them to keep their boat from going over. Below the dam the water was dashing with strong force over great boulders and through crevices in the rocks. Caught by the swirling waters under the rocks, they never came to the surface. After days of relentless searching, the divers finally found one body, and then, two or three days later, the other.[20]

Hebrews readers did not realize they were in danger of drifting away from the Christian faith. Perhaps life was busy. Dust began to pile up on their Scriptures. Missing one or two Sunday assemblies gradually stretched into longer absences. Without the help of God's Word and fellowship, they grew spiritually weak. When persecution came, they had no strength to stand. It was tempting to leave the faith and return to the comfortable Old Law of Judaism.

How do Bible knowledge, regular worship, and
fellowship provide strength during persecution?

Spiritual weakness from a lack of study and fellowship leads to sin. It can happen to any of us. We begin to neglect God's instructions and commit sin. There are consequences. This was true even under the old Jewish covenant.

People living under the Law of Moses who committed "sins of transgression" (doing what God said not to do) and "sins of disobedience" (not doing what He said to do), received severe penalties (Numbers 15:30-31). The Hebrews writer asserted that if those people were punished, the same would happen to Christians who neglected the better faith. "Neglect" here (*ameleo*) means "to be careless about."[21]

Contrast the term "neglect" in verse 3 with the term "earnest" in verse 1.

Jesus illustrated such disregard for the kingdom in His parable of the marriage feast (Matthew 22:1-14). The Old Testament laws, given through prophets and angels (Acts 7:52-53), were as binding during that period as the New Testament is today. God has always demanded obedience. Christians will not escape punishment if we "neglect" the great salvation God has granted under the new covenant.

Sisters, do you know people who call themselves Christians but do no more than sit in the pew? Our journey calls for much more! We must dig deeply in His Word and grow (2 Peter 3:18). We must be light, salt, and servants of God. We must bring the lost to Jesus (Matthew 28:19-20). Yes, Christianity requires more than the Law of Moses, but it promises better rewards (Hebrews 8:6; 10:35). It offers a great inheritance because it was purchased at a great price—the blood of Christ—and it is the only hope of salvation (Acts 4:12). Lightfoot warned, "How unthinkable that men should ignore their sole means of deliverance."[22]

Yes, it is unthinkable that these Hebrew Christians (or we) should reject God's great plan. When presented by His Son and His apostles, it was confirmed with miracles, such as healing the sick, mastery over nature, and gifts of tongues and prophecy (Mark 16:20). The Hebrews writer and his readers had been convinced by eyewitnesses that the Lord's message was true.[23] How then could they—how can we—have flippantly disregarded His instructions?

The Jewish converts started out spiritually strong, but they had begun a downward spiral, drifting from the better path. The writer's concern shows in the first of five warnings in his letter. Each becomes stronger as the letter progresses:

> > **Do not *drift* from the Word—Hebrews 2:1-4 (neglect)**
> - Do not *doubt* the Word—Hebrews 3:7–4:13 (hard heart)
> - Do not become *dull* toward the Word—Hebrews 5:11–6:20 (sluggishness)
> - Do not *despise* the Word—Hebrews 10:26-39 (willfulness)
> - Do not *defy* the Word—Hebrews 12:25-29 (refusing to hear)[24]

Slow and imperceptible drifting from God's Word occurs today. Sisters, we still need the message of Hebrews. It reminds us that Jesus and the path He provided are better than any other faith because they provide the one and only way to be saved.

---

*List some things Christians may do or neglect
to do that could lead to drifting from the faith.*

JESUS CAME TO CLEAR THE WAY (HEBREWS 2:5-16)

Did you find Hebrews 2:1-4 to be a good conclusion to chapter 1? *Because* God has spoken to us by His Son (1:2), *therefore,* we must obey His confirmed Word. To neglect it poses the danger of drifting away.

The rest of Hebrews 2 explains why Jesus came to earth. We use the term "incarnation," meaning "the embodiment of a deity or spirit in some earthly form."[25] Jesus came to become the *archegos* (author, pioneer; v. 10), a word chosen by the writer to portray Him as the "one who trod this earthly way before us as he established the way of salvation."[26]

Jesus became human to clear the path for our journey to a better place.

Satan works to confuse people about the Lord. Some in the first century, as today, rejected Jesus' deity and believed He was only a man. On the other extreme, some taught Docetism, the theory that Jesus was totally divine and only *appeared* to be human (not really flesh and blood). Others taught that He was an angel. So the writer began this letter by confirming Jesus' deity and supremacy over the angels. Now he explained why it was necessary for the Lord to live as a human. Leon Morris noted,

> There was nothing about the Teacher from Nazareth to show that he was greater than the angels. Indeed, the opposite was true, for he had undergone humiliating sufferings culminating in a felon's death. The author proceeds to show, however, that, far from this being an objection to his greatness, this was part of it. This was the way he would save men. He would be made like those he saves.[27]

How blessed we are that our Lord stepped down from heaven's riches to become a pauper on earth! How thankful we should be that He accepted suffering and death to

Jesus came to become the archegos, a word chosen by the writer to portray Him as the "one who trod this earthly way before us as he established the way of salvation."

empathize with us and pave the way for our salvation! To do this, He had to live on earth as a real human.

Read the words of a favorite hymn that expresses this concept such as "Why Did My Savior Come to Earth?"

Human Glory and Honor Restored (Hebrews 2:5-9)

5 *For He has not put the world to come, of which we speak, in subjection to angels.* **6** *But one testified in a certain place, saying: "What is man that You are mindful of him, or the son of man that You take care of him,* **7** *You have made him a little [while] lower than the angels; You have crowned him with glory and honor, and set him over the works of Your hands.* **8** *You have put all things in subjection under his feet." For in that He put all in subjection under him, He left nothing that is not put under him. But now we do not yet see all things put under him.* **9** *But we see Jesus, who was made a little lower than the angels, for the suffering of death crowned with glory and honor, that He, by the grace of God, might taste death for everyone.*

In Hebrews 2:5-9, the writer confirmed that God sent His Son to become a human and to have dominion over the earth. Angels never held that authority, but at creation, such power was given to humans. When God made male and female, He placed them in a unique position: a little lower than the angels, but supreme over "every living thing that moves on the earth" (Genesis 1:28).

David expressed awe at this concept in Psalm 8:4-5: "What is man that You are mindful of him, and the son of man that You visit him? For You have made him a little lower than the angels, and You have crowned him with glory and honor."[28] Adam and Eve were blessed with great human glory and honor. But when they disobeyed God and let sin into the world, the human condition changed. Lightfoot wrote: "God, mindful of man from the beginning, gave him a high place. He bestowed on him glory and honor and made him lord of creation (Gen.1:26-28). All things were put under his feet. But man rebelled and lost his universal dominion."[29]

After the fall, we no longer had full dominion, and we became subject to elements like disease and death. The resulting daily trials make our journey here on earth difficult. Have you not wished Eve had listened more attentively to God's word? One scholar noted our frustrating "equivalents of the 'thorns and thistles' (Gen.3:18) that make life so hard for the tiller of the soil." [30]

Read Genesis 3:14-21, and list the
consequences of this first sin in the garden.

God had a plan to restore human glory and honor in "the world to come" (Hebrews 2:5). This term described the period of Jesus' reign. Ancient Jews divided time into two ages: (1) the time of the old covenant, in which they lived, and (2) the better, future age of the Messiah, whom they never envisioned as a suffering servant. This second period began on the Day of Pentecost, when the gospel was preached concerning Jesus' death, burial, and resurrection. It is the Christian age in which the first-century readers were living and in which we live today (6:5).

Psalm 8 was not just about man. It was a prophecy about Jesus. The Hebrews writer did not name the text quoted. Readers knew that the one who "testified" was David and that the "certain place" was Psalm 8. They also knew this referred to the Messiah. Would it not be wonderful if all of us knew the Old Testament that well?

The prophecy explained that God sent His Son from heaven and made Him temporarily "a little lower than the angels," like us. His purpose was to die on the cross and make salvation possible for all. Afterward, Jesus was "crowned with glory and honor" (Hebrews 2:9; Philippians 2:8-9), and now He sits at the right hand of God.

All of this was in God's mind before the foundation of the world (1 Peter 1:20). He gave a glimpse of the plan of salvation to Adam and Eve in the garden. After their disobedient act, they stood before Him sinful and exposed, except for a few fig leaves. To cover their nakedness, God made clothing of animal skins. This was the first of a repetitive shedding of animals' blood to cover sin. Adam and his descendants were instructed to offer animal sacrifices until the perfect Lamb came and shed His blood on our behalf. This is why Jesus came to earth.

> *A Holy Brotherhood (Hebrews 2:10-13)*
> **10** *For it was fitting for Him, for whom are all things and by whom are all things, in bringing many sons to glory, to make the captain of their salvation perfect through sufferings.* **11** *For both He who sanctifies and those who are being sanctified are all of one, for which reason He is not ashamed to call them brethren,* **12** *saying: "I will declare Your name to My brethren; in the midst of the assembly I will sing praise to You."* **13** *And again: "I will put My trust in Him." And again: "Here am I and the children whom God has given Me."*

I remember as a little girl being encouraged by the sentiment "You are a child of the King, and that makes you a princess." While the definition of princess may be debated today, being a child of God is a wonderful reality! It is shown in the words of one of my favorite hymns: "God is my Father and Jesus is my Brother ... we are members of the family of God." The Hebrews writer emphasized this truth in Hebrews 2:10-13. These verses reveal several aspects of the special relationship we share with God's Son.

First, we share humanity. The Jews had anticipated a different kind of Messiah—a military-like general who would reestablish the great earthly kingdom of Israel. It was difficult for them to understand why God would send a humble servant like Jesus to die on a cross. Hebrews 2:10 clarifies that it was fitting (appropriate) for God, who made all things and in whom all things exist, to make His Son go through the human maturity process ("perfection"). Was Jesus not already perfect? Yes, but as Hebrews will later explain more fully, He had to walk in our shoes in order to clear the path for our salvation.

His experiences with suffering allowed Him to understand our struggles. This is huge because empathy was an essential trait for His heavenly roles as our Mediator and High Priest. Two Old Testament texts (quoted in Hebrews 2:13) express this camaraderie: "I will put My trust in Him" and "Here am I and the children whom God has given Me." The first, from 2 Samuel 22:3, reveals Jesus' dependence on God while enduring human trials and temptations. The second, from Isaiah 8:18, conveys our relationship as "children" given to Him just as the disciples were (John 17:6).

Second, we share a loving Father. God sent Jesus to bring many "sons to glory." Sons, here, refers to followers of God. Glory means "the splendor of ultimate salvation."[31] Thus, "sons of glory" are Christians following God. These words offered encouragement to these Jewish converts. As is true of all the faithful, they would one day share in the glory Jesus was given after His suffering. Nothing in Judaism could have compared with this spiritual reward.

As sons (and daughters), we need to know our Father. Jesus revealed God's character in His actions, attitudes, and teachings. The Hebrews writer quoted from the messianic psalm: "I will declare Your name to My brethren" (Hebrews 2:12; cf. Psalm 22:22). And when two or three of us are gathered together, He is with us (Matthew 18:20). Sisters, it should significantly affect our worship to hear Him say, "In the midst of the assembly I will sing praise to You."

---

*How should Jesus' presence in
our assembly affect our worship?*

Third, we share in holiness (sanctification). Readers knew this term. In the old Jewish system, people, places, and things were often sanctified—that is, made holy, "set apart from a common to a sacred use."[32]

Hebrews 2:11 reveals that Jesus (who is holy, cf. 7:26) sanctifies those who follow Him. We are set apart from the world in a special relationship of "oneness" with God's Son.

Jesus calls us spiritual siblings! He is not ashamed of this solidarity. We should not be ashamed to claim Him. This may have been a weakness for some readers. Jews who converted to Christianity were rejected, both by those

"Sanctified," an important word used often by the Hebrews writer, means made holy, "set apart from a common to a sacred use."

still in Judaism and by those in the world. This letter reminded them that they were part of a wonderful, better spiritual family. We are too. May this reality encourage us.

> *Satan's Power Has Been Diminished (Hebrews 2:14-16)*
> **14** *Inasmuch then as the children have partaken of flesh and blood, He Himself likewise shared in the same, that through death He might destroy him who had the power of death, that is, the devil,* **15** *and release those who through fear of death were all their lifetime subject to bondage.* **16** *For indeed He does not give aid to angels, but He does give aid to the seed of Abraham.*

At the time Hebrews was written, persecution was escalating. Satan used fear of death to control and weaken Christians. Readers needed reminding that Jesus had walked this way before and had cleared the path.

By His death and resurrection, Jesus victoriously fulfilled God's promise in the garden to crush Satan's head. This destroyed Satan's power over the last enemy—death (1 Corinthians 15:26). By sharing this human experience and overcoming it, Jesus paved the way for our resurrection (Revelation 1:18). Thus, we have hope of eternal life. We need not fear death (14:13). Thompson beautifully summarized,

> Through the resurrection, the fear of death is removed. According to 1 Corinthians 15:20, Christ is merely the "first fruits" of a general resurrection for the righteous. In Hebrews, the thought of Christ as pioneer (vs.10) is still in mind. The word for deliver (*apallasso*) is the word that was used for delivering people from a siege. The fear of death had held men in bondage. By experiencing and overcoming death, Christ rescues men from this fear.[33]

Why do some fear death? Why should Christians look forward to it?

In our Christian journey, Jesus gives aid. The Greek term means "to take by the hand," as God led the Israelites out of Egypt to the Promised Land.[34] As the spiritual seed of Abraham ("those who are of faith," Galatians 3:7), we receive special guidance and protection. Not even the angels have this blessing! How comforting this must have been to readers facing persecution and temptation to forsake the Lord. What comfort it brings to us!

> *Jesus Became Our High Priest (Hebrews 2:17-18)*
> **17** *Therefore, in all things He had to be made like His brethren, that He might be a merciful and faithful High Priest in things pertaining to God, to make propitiation for the sins of the people.* **18** *For in that He Himself has suffered, being tempted, He is able to aid those who are tempted.*

In Judaism, the high priest fulfilled two important responsibilities: (1) representing God to man and man to God and (2) offering sacrifices. Jesus had to become flesh to be qualified in these roles as our great High Priest.

We have already noted that Jesus represented God to us when He walked the earth, but because He lived as a human, He is also better able to intercede on our behalf (represent us) to God. Thus, Jesus is qualified to be our merciful and faithful High Priest. Concerning the sacrifice (Leviticus 16:16), Jesus fulfilled this far better than animals in the Jewish system. He not only made the offering; He *was* the offering. His blood provides propitiation (covering) for our sins (Romans 3:25; 1 John 2:2). Human priests and their sacrifices fell short. Compared to both entities in the Jewish religion—the high priest and his sacrifice— Jesus is better!

How did Jesus' life on earth make Him a better High Priest for us?

SUMMARY AND LOOKING FORWARD TO THE NEXT CHAPTER

Jesus lived as a human in order to fulfill God's plan for our salvation. Hebrews warns readers not to drift away but, instead, to follow the way He prepared. As sanctified sons and daughters of glory, we need not fear death but should look forward to our resurrection in a better place. We have help from our Lord, whose sacrificial death on the cross was the pinnacle of His incarnational work and whose sufferings qualified Him to be our High Priest. He now sits with us in worship, continually covers our sins, and leads us by the hand as we take this earthly journey. In Hebrews 3, we will see a warning to readers not to imitate their ancestors in ancient Israel. That generation drifted from and doubted God's word and eventually failed to finish their journey to a better place.

CHAPTER 3

PERSEVERE TO THE END
(HEBREWS 3)

W
e all love happy endings. In *Love Comes Softly*, Marty struggled through the loss of her husband, but a new love came that renewed her dreams for a better life. And Laura Ingalls' weekly adventures in *Little House* always left us smiling. In such stories, heroes and heroines overcome their obstacles and persevere to the happy end. They reach the goal in their journey to a better place.

But this does not always happen in real life. Sometimes travelers fall short of their destination. This is what happened to ancestors of the Jewish Christians. Israel's first generation out of Egypt did not reach the Promised Land. In the Hebrews letter, readers were warned not to imitate these forefathers. As Christians, they had a better leader than Moses and a better promised land than Canaan.

> *A Leader Superior to Moses (Hebrews 3:1-6)*
> **1** *Therefore, holy brethren, partakers of the heavenly calling, consider the Apostle and High Priest of our confession, Christ Jesus,* **2** *who was faithful to Him who appointed Him, as Moses also was faithful in all His house.* **3** *For this One has been counted worthy of more glory than Moses, inasmuch as He who built the house has more honor than the house.* **4** *For every house is built by someone, but He who built all things is God.* **5** *And Moses indeed was faithful in all His house as a servant, for a testimony of those things which would be spoken afterward,* **6** *But Christ as a Son over His own house, whose house we are if we hold fast the confidence and the rejoicing of the hope firm to the end.*

Hebrew Christians were familiar with the concept of journeying to a better place. They had grown up hearing about Israel's deliverance from Egypt, Red Sea crossing, and travel to the Promised Land. They also revered the God-sent deliverer of that multitude: Moses. Admiration for this leader made it difficult for some to see him as inferior to Jesus, the head of their new faith. But this was the writer's emphasis in Hebrews 3. Brett R. Scott summarized,

> Moses delivered the Israelites from the bondage of slavery and Egypt, while Jesus delivered all believers from the bondage of sin and damnation (2:14-15). Through Moses, God constituted the Israelites as the people of God, while Jesus constitutes all believers as the sons of God (2:10). Moses brought the Israelites the Old Covenant, whereas Jesus brings all believers into the New Covenant, establishing a greater access to God for them (4:14-16), which had been only for Israel until Jesus came. In Jesus' superiority He replaced—and exceeded—all Moses did.[35]

Through Christ, God gave His final and complete message. This better message annulled the Law of Moses, nailing it to the cross (Colossians 2:14). Jesus leads spiritual Israel (Christians) toward a better promised land. The Hebrews writer here used the title "Christ" (Messiah, the Anointed One) and explained that not even the great Old Testament deliverer Moses was comparable.

In Hebrews 3:1, the writer opened with the word "therefore" once again. Readers must look back at the truths just presented and apply them to what was written next. Jesus, God's Son, is the pioneer of our salvation. He is superior even to the angels. He is also superior to Moses. God appointed both Christ Jesus and Moses to specific tasks. Each was faithful in his role as an "apostle," as the term is defined: "one sent with full authority to represent the sender."[36] But Jesus is better.

An "apostle" is "one sent out with full authority to represent the sender." Using this definition, describe how Moses and, later, Christ fulfilled that role (cf. Exodus 3:7-10; Luke 4:43.)

Christ Jesus serves as our High Priest. Moses never held this position. His brother, Aaron, fulfilled this role in Judaism and offered animals for Israel. If Hebrews readers had fully acknowledged Christ's greatness, they would not have been tempted to return to the Old Law (delivered through Moses). They would have been able to stand against the world's opposition and affirm with their lips that Jesus was the new deliverer and author of salvation (Matthew 10:32-33; 1 Timothy 6:12). The same is true for us, so this letter still serves as a faith-building reminder.

In this section of Hebrews, the writer alluded to the readers' group status as God's household. Israel was His house, and Moses was only a faithful member and servant (Numbers 12:7). That house was a type and shadow (symbol) of the house of the new covenant, the church, of which readers were a part (Ephesians 2:19; 1 Timothy 3:15). The head of this house is Christ (Ephesians 1:22). He is not just a member. He is the Father's Son, and as Hebrews 3:3 states, He "has been counted worthy of more glory than Moses."

Christ Jesus is also the builder of this spiritual house. He revealed to His disciples that upon the truth of His identity as "the Christ, the Son of the living God" He would build His church (Matthew 16:16-18). He carried out that promise at Pentecost (Acts 2). Even before He built the church, Christ was the builder of all things. At creation, the Father spoke, and the Son performed His commands. The Gospel of John explains, "In the beginning was the Word, and the Word was with God, and the Word was God. He was in the beginning with God. All things were made through Him, and without Him nothing was made that was made" (1:1-3). Thus, Christ is superior to Moses. He is "over His own house"—that is, over all people who make up God's spiritual family (Hebrews 3:6).

Christ is greater than Moses. Why was
this reminder important for Jewish readers?

However, like their ancestors, readers were losing confidence in God's promises of care and salvation. The Hebrews writer explained that the privilege of being in God's household is conditional. There is no truth in the concept "once saved, always saved." We can remain in God's house *only* "if we hold fast the confidence and the rejoicing of the hope firm to the end" (Hebrews 3:6). Christians must persevere through the entire journey, even until death. Warren W. Wiersbe explained,

> In other words, those who have trusted Christ prove this confession by their steadfastness, confidence, and joyful hope. They are not burdened by the past or threatened by the present, but are "living in the future tense" as they await the "blessed hope" of their Lord's return. It is this "heavenly calling" that motivates the believers to keep on living for the Savior even when the going is tough.[37]

Faith and conviction are especially needed during trials of life. Here, "confidence" means courage, boldness, and fearlessness. "Rejoicing" implies taking pride in something and having something to boast about. Jews often bragged about being Abraham's seed (cf. John 8:33). But they were more blessed to be his spiritual seed through Christ (Galatians 3:26-29). They should have been proud, not ashamed, to have been members of the church, as we should be. We must boldly proclaim faith, even until death, for that is when the reward is given (Revelation 2:10). Sadly, many leave the path Christ prepared in search of another. This is what the Hebrews writer feared for his readers.

How does the word "if" in Hebrews 3:6
assert that salvation is conditional?

DO NOT DOUBT THE WORD (HEBREWS 3:7-19)

The writer pleaded, "Stay on the better path!" He warned readers about their ancestors who had followed Moses. The multitude began well and worshiped God after crossing the Red Sea, but they lost confidence in God's promises. Even as He provided food, water, and protection, they complained. When He brought them to the edge of the Promised Land, they doubted His assurance of victory. As a result, they did not enter. One writer compared weak Christians "who doubt God's word and live in restless unbelief" to the Israelites wandering in the wilderness; both are "out of Egypt, but not yet in Canaan."[38] Some Christians today exist in similar circumstances. Sisters, do you know any half-hearted members in the church?

Faith comes by hearing God's Word (Romans 10:17). Drifting from His Word naturally leads to doubting it. The second of Hebrews' five warnings is against doubt.

- Do not *drift* from the Word—Hebrews 2:1-4 (neglect)
- > **Do not *doubt* the Word—Hebrews 3:7–4:13 (hard heart)**
- Do not become *dull* toward the Word—Hebrews 5:11–6:20 (sluggishness)
- Do not *despise* the Word—Hebrews 10:26-39 (willfulness)
- Do not *defy* the Word—Hebrews 12:25-29 (refusing to hear)

The writer began this warning in Hebrews 3:7-11 by quoting Psalm 95:7-11. There, David wrote of Israel's rebellion in the wilderness when the ancient Israelites drifted and doubted.

Hardening of the Heart (Hebrews 3:7-11)
7 *Therefore, as the Holy Spirit says: "Today, if you will hear His voice,* **8** *do not harden your hearts as in the rebellion, in the day of trial in the wilderness,* **9** *where your fathers tested Me, tried Me, and saw My works forty years.* **10** *Therefore I was angry with that generation, and said, 'They always go astray in their heart, and they have not known My ways.'* **11** *So I swore in My wrath, 'They shall not enter My rest.'"*

Two incidents of the Israelites' rebellion are referenced in this passage. One took place at Rephidim, near the beginning of their journey to the Promised Land (Exodus 17:1-7). The term "rebellion" refers to the Israelites' murmuring as they asked, "Is the LORD among us or not?" (v. 7). Through Moses, God provided water from a rock. The other incident occurred at Kadesh, near the entrance to the Promised Land

(Numbers 13:25–14:35). The Israelites listened to the report of ten cowardly spies instead of the courageous pleas of Joshua and Caleb. David described them as a people who went astray in their hearts (Psalm 95:10). Sentiments of the heart guide our actions.

Can you see why this letter is easier to understand if you are familiar with the Old Testament? The writer referred to it often. Read each reference in this study guide and develop a greater love for the early chapters of God's old, old story. Let us include that material in our regular Bible study, for it was written for our learning (Romans 15:4). Israel's example shows us that when we neglect Bible study, our faith becomes weak. We begin to drift away from God. We begin to doubt His promises. And we begin to develop a hardened heart.

Deliberate refusal to believe and "stubbornness against listening to and obeying the Lord" describe the condition of a hardened heart.

Thompson defined deliberate refusal to believe as "hardening of the heart ... stubbornness against listening to and obeying the Lord." [39]

The Israelites lost confidence in God's words to them; their hearts became hardened, and they ended their journey. This happens today. Without faith, hearts can become bitter and hardened. One day, two of our sons and their friends were riding with us from school when one of the friends bitterly asked, "What kind of God would let my grandmother die of cancer?" This poor child did not know God or His Word. His heart had already become bitter, and without teaching in love, it could easily become hardened.

---

*How does the study of God's Word
prevent hardening of the heart?*

Scripture teaches that our defense against heart-hardening is confidence in God's Word. Job lost everything, but he continued to trust God (Job 1:21-22). Naomi lost her family, became bitter, and blamed God; but she later allowed His goodness to soften her heart (Ruth 1:20; 2:20). Pharaoh refused to believe God's promise of the plagues, and when they occurred, his heart hardened (Exodus 8:15, 32). The Israelites left Egypt in a state of belief, but they soon doubted and rejected God. Doubters hurt only themselves. Lightfoot wrote about Israel, "They shut themselves out of their promised homeland."[40] Through the pen of inspiration, both David and the Hebrews writer urged God's people in their generations, "Do not harden your hearts as in the rebellion" (Hebrews 3:8). Our generation faces this temptation too. Let us trust God and not become hardened.

The Israelites witnessed the plagues in Egypt, the parting of the Red Sea, the quail, the manna, and the water; but they did not continue to walk in God's ways. He became disgusted with them and proclaimed, "Because all these men who have seen My glory and the signs which I did in Egypt and in the wilderness, and have put Me to the test ... and have not heeded My voice, they certainly shall not see the land of which I swore to their fathers, nor shall any of those who rejected Me see it" (Numbers 14:22-23). As punishment, God made them wander forty years in the wilderness until everyone over the age of twenty at the time of the rebellion (except Joshua and Caleb) died. They never entered the Promised Land rest as they had anticipated (Hebrews 3:11).

Why do you think the Hebrews writer reviewed these
incidences of doubt and God's response in ancient Israel?

Everyone Stay Together (Hebrews 3:12-19)
12 *Beware, brethren, lest there be in any of you an evil heart of unbelief in departing from the living God;* **13** *but exhort one another daily, while it is called "Today," lest any of you be hardened through the deceitfulness of sin.* **14** *For we have become partakers of Christ if we hold the beginning of our confidence steadfast to the end,* **15** *while it is said: "Today, if you will hear His voice, do not harden your hearts as in the rebellion."* **16** *For who, having heard, rebelled? Indeed, was it not all who came out of Egypt, led by Moses?* **17** *Now with whom was He angry forty years? Was it not with those who sinned, whose corpses fell in the wilderness?* **18** *And to whom*

did He swear that they would not enter His rest, but to those who did not obey? 19 So we see that they could not enter in because of unbelief.

Hebrews 3:12-19 urges us to help one another in our journey to a better place. Christianity is an individual walk, but brothers and sisters provide support. We must help one another lest any drift, doubt, and develop a hardened heart.

Perhaps you have heard the illustration about a pile of hot coals from which one is removed and set aside. The question is asked, "What will happen to the isolated coal?" Of course it will lose its heat and grow cold. When we are baptized, we join the "wagon train" of Christians journeying together toward heaven. Those who fall behind and separate from the others more easily become lost or fall prey to enemies. Satan attacks lone Christians. Hebrews instructs us to encourage one another daily. We all know weak and struggling sisters who desperately need uplifting every day. Without help, many begin to drift and doubt.

We have a responsibility to look out for one another. How many sisters in your congregation are hanging on by their spiritual fingernails? Do we notice when one misses a Sunday? Do we care? Do we ask, "How are you?" Are we willing to listen and offer help? The word "exhort" (*parakaleo*) means "appeal to, encourage."[41] We must help one another trust the Lord and stay on the path together. Hebrews 3:14 repeats the message of verse 6 that the Christian life is a shared journey. We have a common partnership with one another (John 17:20-21). We are our sister's keeper. Our shared goal is to persevere in faith all the way to the end.

Hebrews 3:15 repeats the word "today." Every day we face thorns and thistles of life, and every day we need support. So make that call or send that text today. Tomorrow may be too late. Weekly fellowship is not enough. Early Christians met *daily* in one another's homes (Acts 2:44-47). Their relationships helped them remain strong. Hebrews 10:25 explains that the assembly is designed for encouragement. Pace suggested this implies we should "assemble to encourage more and more, not encourage to assemble more and more."[42] Encouragement must occur to keep hearts strong for the journey.

Why are Christians more vulnerable to Satan's darts when
they are alone? Discuss ways we can encourage one another.

David's words are repeated: "Today, if you will hear His voice, do not harden your hearts as in the rebellion" (Hebrews 3:7, 15). Israel doubted God's promises and wanted to go back into the false security of Egypt (Numbers 14:4). The Hebrew Christians, in their spiritual wilderness, were tempted to rebel against the same living God and seek their security in Judaism. But God provided a better guide than Moses: His own Son. Would they learn from Israel's example?

Hebrews 3:16-18 asks three rhetorical questions and provides the obvious answers:

1. *"Who, having heard, rebelled? Indeed, was it not all who came out of Egypt, led by Moses?" (v. 16).* Readers knew that nearly all who came out of Egypt over the age of twenty doubted. Only Joshua and Caleb remained firm in their faith all the way to the end. Not even the great hero Moses was allowed to enter the Promised Land.

2. *"With whom was He angry forty years? Was it not with those who sinned, whose corpses fell in the wilderness?" (v. 17).* Rejecting God's word is sin. God had been patient, but He was disgusted when Israel doubted His promises at Canaan's door. His punishment was swift, harsh, and final. A whole generation died short of their goal.

3. *"To whom did He swear that they would not enter His rest, but to those who did not obey?" (v. 18).* God promised to bring His people into Canaan—if they followed Him. But they doubted. They did not enter into that rest.

Why did God become disgusted with the ancient Israelites?
Discuss the severity of their punishment.

The physical rest Israel looked forward to was the Promised Land. It was a type and shadow of the spiritual rest we find in Christ. God has promised Christians that, when we follow Him, we have rest in this life and eternal rest after we die.

The writer urged Christians not to follow the Israelites' example. In Hebrews 3:19, he restated their sad end: "So we see that they could not enter in because of unbelief." Greek sentences often end with the word most emphasized. This sentence ends with *apistia* (unbelief).[43] Readers needed to beware of Satan's deception. They would not have been better off returning to Judaism. That would have ended their Christian journey, like those "in the rebellion."

How might this chapter's warnings against
doubting God's Word help Christians today?

SUMMARY AND LOOKING FORWARD TO THE NEXT CHAPTER

Jewish converts were encouraged to persevere on the better path prepared by Christ. They were warned not to imitate the ancient Israelites, who doubted God's word and lost their opportunity to enter the Promised Land. The writer quoted David's record of God's anger at their hardened hearts and His declaration: "They shall not enter My rest" (Hebrews 3:11). As Christians, we can persevere to the end if we walk together and leave no one behind. The chapter ends with three questions concerning those who doubted. These, and even Moses, failed to enter the Promised Land. Christ is the better guide! Hebrews 4 continues this discussion and shows concern that readers might also "fall according to the same example of disobedience" and forfeit their rest (Hebrews 4:11).

CHAPTER 4

LOOK FOR A GOOD REST STOP
(HEBREWS 4)

The word "journey" is defined as "an act of traveling from one place to another."[44] Consider your own memorable trips. My husband and I have enjoyed short ones to church members' homes and long ones to mission points overseas. But the journey our boys talk about most was our move from California to South Carolina when they were four, seven, eleven, and thirteen. We listened to Anne Murray songs, dreamed of things we would do in our new home, and enjoyed snacks at rest stops. The boys would jump from the van and run around; my husband, Steven, and I would relax and enjoy the short break from our journey.

God knows the importance of rest. He established a place of repose for Israel and a spiritual respite for all of His children. The Israelites' doubt kept them from entering the Promised Land, but God's heavenly rest remains available for Christians. First-century Jewish converts needed this reminder. Hebrews 4 continues this discussion.

ISRAEL MISSED GOD'S REST (HEBREWS 4:1-7)

Like the Israelites, these Christians were drifting. They had become weary, discouraged, and apathetic. Their lack of faith had put them in danger of missing the heavenly rest, an outcome the Hebrews writer desperately wanted to avoid.

The Promised Land: A Type of God's Future Rest (Hebrews 4:1-3)
1 *Therefore, since a promise remains of entering His rest, let us fear lest any of you seem to have come short of it.* **2** *For indeed the gospel was preached to us as well as to them; but the word which they heard did not profit them, not being mixed with faith in those who heard it.* **3** *For we who have believed do enter that rest, as He has said: "So I swore in My wrath, 'They shall not enter My rest,'" although the works were finished from the foundation of the world.*

The ancient Israelites anticipated rest in the Promised Land, but their unbelief prevented them from entering. The physical land of Canaan was part of the promise—a land that the second generation of Israel later possessed—but there was more. Canaan was only a type and shadow of the *spiritual* resting place God was preparing for His people. That rest was available for ancient Israel. It was available for first-century readers, and it remains for Christians today. Yet some still fail to reach it, for it is awarded only to those who persevere to the end.

Because of unbelief, first-generation Israelites lost both rests. They heard and accepted the good news of God's covenant promises with an emphasis on Canaan. But when ten spies said "we cannot take the land," the people chose not to try. Faith is shown by actions (James 2:17, 20). The Israelites' lack of action revealed their lack of faith. Lenski noted that "they *heard* the promise of God's rest, all that the glad tidings about this rest contained, but they hardened their hearts (3:8, etc.), they refused to *believe* and thus lost both the earthly and the heavenly Canaan."[45] Doubt was the root of their tragic loss. Doubt can ruin one's Christian journey today.

Hebrews 4:3 explains that all who live in the Christian age and hear the good news (gospel) of Christ have an opportunity to attain the better, eternal rest. The writer included himself with fellow believers who enter that Christian journey at baptism. This immersion in water is a reenactment of Christ's death, burial, and resurrection (Romans 6:3-6). It is at this point when one joins the journey to that better place. However, the promised rest is only for those who remain faithful to the end. If we leave the faith and quit the journey, we miss the rest.

This message encourages every generation of Christians to keep on keeping on. All begin the pilgrimage with joy, but trials and disappointments can discourage. Ancient Israel lost faith, the Hebrews readers wavered, and many today need reminding that doubters shall not enter into God's rest.

Name the two rests ancient Israel missed. How might this message have benefitted first-century Jewish readers? Is it helpful to you?

The Sabbath: A Type of God's Future Rest (Hebrews 4:4-7)
4 For He has spoken in a certain place of the seventh day in this way: "And God rested on the seventh day from all His works"; 5 and again in this place: "They shall not enter My rest." 6 Since therefore it remains that some must enter it, and those to whom it was first preached did not enter because of disobedience, 7 again He designates a certain day, saying in David, "Today," after such a long time, as it has been said: "Today, if you will hear His voice, do not harden your hearts."

After this declaration, the writer alluded to what God did after His work of creation (Hebrews 4:3). It involved another type of rest: the Sabbath. Readers were familiar with the Sabbath and its establishment as a "sign" of eternal rest in which God's people would join Him (Genesis 2:2; Exodus 31:16-17).[46] Under the Law of Moses, Israel enjoyed this weekly respite from physical labor. The Sabbath, as well as physical Canaan, was a type of the "future rest that all believers will enjoy with God" (cf. Hebrews 4:9).[47] John spoke of this rest in Revelation 14:13: "Blessed are the dead who die in the Lord from now on ... that they may rest from their labors, and their works follow them." Christians look forward to that better place.

In Hebrews 4:5-7, the writer again referred to Israel's unbelief and failure to enter God's rest. He quoted Psalm 95:7-11, David's warning to Israel many generations after God first swore, "They shall not enter My rest." Even as David and his kingdom possessed the physical land of Canaan, they had not yet entered into God's "future rest." That future rest is heaven! David's warning to his people reaches across generations to assure readers, "It remains that some must enter it" (Hebrews 4:6). The term "today" was used again to emphasize urgency. Paul proclaimed, "Behold, now is the accepted time; behold, now is the day of salvation" (2 Corinthians 6:2).

Even after obedience to the gospel, salvation is conditional. Only those who persevere to the end of life will enter that blessed rest. Hebrews readers were still on their spiritual journey. It was difficult. Some were drifting, doubting, and in danger of missing their anticipated rest, as are many today. Sisters, will we waver and harden our hearts, or will we persevere in faith and obedience? Will we remain on our heavenward journey and enter the future eternal rest?

How does God's promise of eternal
rest help you persevere in Christianity?

A Better Rest (Hebrews 4:8-10)
8 *For if Joshua had given them rest, then He would not afterward have spoken of another day.* **9** *There remains therefore a rest for the people of God.* **10** *For he who has entered His rest has himself also ceased from his works as God did from His.*

Second-generation Israelites learned from their parents' example and entered the Promised Land (Joshua 22:4). Hebrews 4:8-10 briefly refers to Moses' successor, who led them into this physical land of rest. However, the temporary rest provided by Joshua does not compare with the true eternal rest that Jesus offers.

Joshua was a model of faith and perseverance. He inspired courage in Israel by declaring, "Choose for yourselves this day whom you will serve. ... But as for me and my house, we will serve the LORD" (Joshua 24:15). His example motivated others, even after his death: "Israel served the LORD all the days of Joshua, and all the days of the elders who outlived Joshua, who had known all the works of the LORD which He had done for Israel" (v. 31). Yet compared to Christ Jesus, Joshua provided only a temporary, inferior rest. Lightfoot pointed out,

Joshua was the commander under whose leadership the Israelites entered Canaan. Jesus is the Leader and Pioneer of faith for His people. But the rest that Joshua gave to his followers was only physical; it was only temporary and it did not really satisfy. If it had been adequate, the psalm would not speak about another day. Jesus, however, it is implied, is able to lead His own to their eternal destination.[48]

The future rest of which David and the Hebrews writer spoke is the eternal, heavenly home. Hebrews 4:9-10 explains that it is offered to "the people of God," and in it, each ceases from his labors. Thompson summarized, "This rest has been available since the creation, but never before Christ has it been entered by men. This rest is God's ultimate promise to his people; it will be realized at the end when his people share with God 'a better country, a heavenly one' (11:16)."[49] Let each of us take seriously our responsibility to persevere faithfully so that we can enjoy our blessed rest in that better place.

What made Joshua a good leader? Compare the rest
he provided for Israel with the rest Jesus provides for us.

God's Word Reveals the Heart (Hebrews 4:11-13)
11 *Let us therefore be diligent to enter that rest, lest anyone fall according to the same example of disobedience.* **12** *For the word of God is living and powerful, and sharper than any two-edged sword, piercing even to the division of soul and spirit, and of joints and marrow, and is a discerner of the thoughts and intents of the heart.* **13** *And there is no creature hidden from His sight, but all things are naked and open to the eyes of Him to whom we must give account.*

Completing a journey does not happen unless our heart is in it. If we are not serious in our Christian pilgrimage, we are susceptible to drifting and doubting. However, the Hebrews writer pleaded *because* we have the example of the Israelites forfeiting their rest and *because* it is still available, let us therefore seek to enter that rest and not fail because of disobedience (Hebrews 4:11).

The phrase translated "be diligent" is from *spoudazo*, meaning "be zealous," "make every effort."[50] One cannot make the narrow Christian

The phrase translated "be diligent" means to "be zealous" or to "make every effort."

journey halfheartedly. Paul explained his own diligence in pressing toward the heavenly goal (Philippians 3:14). Nothing is more worthy of our time and energy. Pace commented, "We strive because the prize of eternal redemption is such a glorious one, and the peril of losing it is so great and horrible."[51]

Due to a lack of diligence, the Israelites suffered a terrible loss, and their dead bodies fell in the wilderness (Numbers 14:26-33). The Hebrews writer did not want his readers to fail. Those who do not learn from history are doomed to repeat it. This is true in our local congregations. Thompson suggested that a church "not rooted in its past will have no resources for countering the inevitable frustrations and disappointments of the Christian life. Without our roots in the past experiences of the people of God, we are most likely to repeat their mistakes" and end up just like ancient Israel.[52] We must all learn from mistakes in our own lives and congregations. The unbelief of first-generation Israel and of some in our own church history are examples of what not to do.

What lessons have been learned from mistakes in your congregation's history?

Readers were drifting and doubting because their lack of study had weakened their faith. They were not meditating on Old Testament warnings, promises, and prophecies about Jesus. Therefore, they needed reminding that God's word, which brought forth creation and a covenant relationship with Israel, is just as living and powerful in the Christian age.

Diligent study of the Scriptures is the way to encourage perseverance and to revitalize an apathetic congregation. Some try to revive members through entertainment-oriented worship and charismatic orators teaching watered-down doctrine. Thompson wrote, "Instead of seeing the Word of God as the *answer* for a dying church, many today suspect that it is the *cause* for much of our apathy. ... For us, the Bible has become irrelevant, tedious, and boring."[53] God's Word is neither dead nor irrelevant; it is living and powerful! It guides, encourages, strengthens, comforts, transforms, and makes known the way of salvation.

God's Word also reveals attitudes of the heart. It is described as a "two-edged sword" (Hebrews 4:12), penetrating the two layers of humanity. One layer is called the soul or "psyche"—literally "that which animates the body ... the seat of the thoughts, emotions, feelings ... pertaining to our earthly and bodily existence."[54] The other is the spirit or "pneuma"—the more divine part of our nature,[55] the "immaterial part of our being that was created and breathed into us by the breath of God."[56] This metaphorically reveals how God's Word pierces and exposes heart attitudes. Thomas Hewitt clarified,

> It penetrates into the deepest and most hidden parts of a man's life and dissects his lower animal life with its desires, interests, and affections from his higher spiritual life with its aspirations for spiritual communion with God, just as a two-edged sword cuts through *the joints and marrow* of a physical body. It does not look upon outward appearances but is skilled in judging *the thoughts and intentions of the heart.*[57]

Our omniscient God and His Word search our innermost secrets (1 Chronicles 28:9; Psalm 139:1-2). Our hearts are laid bare, meaning "naked and exposed, stripped of every possible concealment."[58] This idea referred to the sacrificial animal whose neck was pulled back for the knife. Our hearts are always exposed to God. We cannot hide doubt and disbelief.

On judgment day, our lives will be compared to the standard of God's Word. We must daily examine ourselves in its light. If we are not right, His Word confronts us and calls us to repentance and accountability.[59] This is what happened on Pentecost when hearers of the first gospel sermon were "cut to the heart," asked how to be saved, and then were baptized (Acts 2:37-41). Only by obeying God's living and powerful Word can we begin and continue the journey to that better place. Those who resist Scripture have no escape. Indifference and disobedience will cause us to fail as Israel did, and we, too, will miss God's eternal rest. The Hebrews writer was very concerned. Lightfoot asserted,

> The thought—so tragic and horrible when he realizes that the same fate might befall any Christian—never leaves him. So he pleads with his readers that they pay attention to the all-powerful message of God's word and that they remember that they always remain within the scope of the divine gaze. And for their aid he points them to Jesus, their great high priest, and to the throne in heaven that is distinguished by grace.[60]

Explain the concept of God's Word as a two-edged sword
and how it motivates sincerity in the Christian life.

Our High Priest Is Our Help (Hebrews 4:14-16)
14 Seeing then that we have a great High Priest who has passed through the heavens, Jesus the Son of God, let us hold fast our confession. 15 For we do not have a High Priest who cannot sympathize with our weaknesses, but was in all points tempted as we are, yet without sin. 16 Let us therefore come boldly to the throne of grace, that we may obtain mercy and find grace to help in time of need.

Hebrews 4:14 turns attention back to Christ Jesus. He sits at God's right hand, serving as a representative of God to man and an advocate for man to God. The reality of His high priesthood is the theme of this letter and the focus of its center (Hebrews 4:14–10:18).

As High Priest, Christ helps us, especially during difficult and discouraging times in our Christian journey. We can draw comfort from Hebrews 4:14-16. Whatever trials we have, Jesus has been there and done that. He understands and empathizes. He explains our situation to the Father, and we receive the mercy, grace, and help we need any time.

Some first-century readers questioned Jesus' messiahship and felt a need for the familiar Jewish high priest. In their former religion, they watched this human pass through the veil into the temple sanctuary.

But in this Most Holy Place, he alone could enter God's presence. Readers needed reminding that, when Jesus died, God ripped its veil from top to bottom and opened up a new avenue by which we can all approach the Father (Matthew 27:51).

This new avenue is Christ Jesus. He passed through the heavens and now sits at God's right hand as our eternal High Priest. He is not like those in Aaron's lineage who served only Jews. He is an advocate for all God's children. It is His name we confess at baptism, and it is that confession of faith to which we must remain steadfast. Jesus promised that if we confess His name on earth, He will confess ours in heaven (Matthew 10:32-33). No such promise existed in the Jewish religion.

As our High Priest, Christ is our indispensable help. He understands our weaknesses—physical, emotional, and spiritual. He walked in our shoes. He felt the nails in His hands, the sorrow of losing a loved one, and all the fiery darts of Satan. He was "in all points tempted as we are" by the lust of the flesh, the lust of the eyes, and the pride of life (Hebrews 4:15; 1 John 2:16). Yet He did not sin (2 Corinthians 5:21; 1 Peter 2:21-22).

We cannot be sinless, but with God's help, we can sin less. We can memorize scripture as an aid: "Thy word have I hid in mine heart, that I might not sin against thee" (Psalm 119:11 KJV). We can resist the devil, and he will flee from us (James 4:7). We can begin each day in prayer: "Do not lead us into temptation, but deliver us from the evil one" (Matthew 6:13). A humorous morning prayer goes like this: "Dear God, so far today I've done all right. I haven't gossiped, been greedy, grumpy, nasty, selfish, or over-indulgent. I'm really glad about that, but in a few minutes, God, I'm going to get out of bed, and from then on, I'm probably going to need a lot more help!" Sisters, when we awaken and first pray, we will enjoy a better day.

Jesus' experience as a frail, earthly human qualified Him to be our advocate, our great High Priest. Hebrews 4:16 urges, "Let us therefore come boldly to the throne of grace." The term "boldly" meant "the right of a full citizen to speak his mind on any subject in the town assembly— a right that the slave did not have."[61] Lightfoot noted, "In the Epistle it stands for freedom to approach God on the basis of the blood of Jesus (10:19)."[62] Those who have been washed in Christ's blood have the right to draw near to God. From His throne, He dispenses mercy and grace when we need it.

Name some blessings we have in Jesus Christ as our High Priest.

SUMMARY AND LOOKING FORWARD TO THE NEXT CHAPTER

What a blessing Christians have to anticipate a future, eternal rest with God! We have biblical examples such as Israel's failure and Joshua's success. In our journey, we can draw knowledge, encouragement, and comfort from God's powerful Word. It is the standard by which we will be judged. In this life, we have an advocate in Christ Jesus. The next chapter, Hebrews 5, continues to focus on our great High Priest. Through Him, we can come boldly to the throne of God and get the help we need. We should take advantage of this privilege in our journey to a better place.

CHAPTER 5

ARE WE THERE YET?
(HEBREWS 5)

O ur family journey from California to South Carolina was a five-day adventure. We traveled through Arizona and New Mexico for the first time, spent a day with my grandmother in Arlington, Texas, and experienced the beauty and hospitality of the Southeast in which I grew up. But it was a long trip, and though we tried to make it interesting, our youngest often asked the famous childhood question: "Are we there yet?" Most children are too young to understand travel time and distance. It takes maturity to comprehend many of life's concepts.

The same is true for new Christians on their spiritual journeys. They love Jesus and enjoy His blessings, yet many struggle on the path to spiritual maturity and wonder why they aren't there yet. That path requires deep Bible study, without which one cannot comprehend God's most profound truths.

In Hebrews 5, the writer introduced one of those truths: Christ's priesthood. He later rebuked readers' spiritual stagnation, which had rendered them unable to grasp it. He knew they needed to understand Jesus' superiority because, by not doing so, some looked back to the Jewish priesthood. James Burton Coffman wrote,

> Without doubt, the earthly splendor of the Jewish high priest was a factor of seductive influence on Christians, especially those of Jewish background. His rich robes, the extravagantly ornate breastplate, the unique privilege of entering the holy of holies on the day of atonement, his status as judge and president of the Sanhedrin, his dramatic

influence as the official representative of the Jewish nation, more especially at a time when they had no king, the traditional descent of the
office from the sons of Aaron and reaching all the way back to the Exodus, and the grudging respect paid to the office, even by the Roman
conquerors—all these things and many others elevated the Jewish high
priest to a position of isolated splendor in the eyes of the people.[63]

However, in God's plan of salvation, earthly priests were no longer
needed. In fact, when Hebrews was written, the temple and its sacrificial system were about to come to an end (Hebrews 12:26-27; Matthew 24:15-22).[64] Readers needed encouragement to rely on Jesus as
the great High Priest of which the Old Testament priesthood was just
a type. This chapter reveals His qualifications as a better High Priest.

A BETTER HIGH PRIEST (HEBREWS 5:1-10)

Better than Earthly High Priests (Hebrews 5:1-3)
*1 For every high priest taken from among men is appointed for men in
things pertaining to God, that he may offer both gifts and sacrifices for
sins. 2 He can have compassion on those who are ignorant and going
astray, since he himself is also subject to weakness. 3 Because of this he is
required as for the people, so also for himself, to offer sacrifices for sins.*

When God established the Jewish priesthood in the Law of Moses,
He chose Aaron and his descendants to fulfill the "things pertaining to
God" (Hebrews 5:1; cf. Exodus 28:1). Their duties included offering
gifts and sacrifices for sin. The gifts were inanimate offerings, such as
oil, grain, and incense. The sacrifices were animals, such as bulls and
rams. Human priests ministered on behalf of all Israelites, including
themselves, for they, too, were sinners in need of forgiveness (Leviticus
16:6). Hebrews 5 opens with these truths.

Acknowledging their own weaknesses promoted compassion, a
quality required in priests. It was necessary for them to deal gently with
people. They had to discern between ignorant, wayward sinners and
the rebellious. Atonement could be made for the former, but not for
those who committed sins presumptuously (Leviticus 5:14-16; Numbers 15:28-31). The "forgivable" list included sins of passion. For ex-

ample, Aaron made the golden calf in the midst of chaotic frenzy. He was forgiven and later appointed as high priest. Jesus met and exceeded these qualifications to be our High Priest.

Earlier we read, "Therefore, in all things He had to be made like His brethren, that He might be a merciful and faithful High Priest in things pertaining to God, to make propitiation for the sins of the people. For in that He Himself has suffered, being tempted, He is able to aid those who are tempted" (Hebrews 2:17-18). Our Lord lived as a human in order to represent God to us and to be our advocate to the Father. He performed the high priest's duty of making a sin offering on our behalf. He volunteered Himself as the perfect, unblemished sacrifice. It was truly redemptive because it made animal sacrifices and earthly priests no longer necessary.

Compare this earlier reading (Hebrews 2:17-18) with Hebrews 5:1, and discuss Jesus' qualifications as High Priest.

Jesus was tempted as we are, but without sin. This produced a unique empathy within Him for our human situations, and along with the priestly requirement of compassion, He became qualified as our merciful and faithful High Priest. We see this in His prayer for those who crucified Him: "Father, forgive them, for they do not know what they do" (Luke 23:34). Most were ignorant and caught up in the passion of the moment. Some later repented and were baptized (Acts 2:36-41). Jesus fulfills the role of high priest better than any human ever could. In addition, His was a better appointment, for He was called by God.

Called by God (Hebrews 5:4-5)

4 *And no man takes this honor to himself, but he who is called by God, just as Aaron was.* 5 *So also Christ did not glorify Himself to become High Priest, but it was He who said to Him: "You are My Son, today I have begotten You."*

The original readers might have smiled as they heard the words "no man takes this honor to himself." They knew of egotistical men who grabbed the position of high priest through force, bribery, and political favors. They had read of corrupt priests (Malachi 1:7-8) and others who unlawfully practiced priestly roles (King Saul, 1 Samuel 13:8-14). First-century historian Josephus wrote about examples of unlawful political appointees closer to their own time:

> So king Herod immediately took the high priesthood away from Anan-elus, ... though what he did was plainly unlawful, for at no other time [of old] was any one that had once been in that dignity deprived of it. It was Antiochus Epiphanes who first brake that law, and deprived Jesus, and made his brother Onias high priest in his stead. Aristobulus was the second that did so, and took that dignity from his brother [Hyrcanus]; and this Herod was the third, who took that high office away [from Arianflus], and gave it to this young man, Aristobulus, in his stead.[65]

Therefore, along with Jesus' empathetic and sacrificial qualifications, the Hebrews writer presented the fact that His high priesthood was appointed by God. Our Lord did not seek honor for Himself, only glorification for the Father (John 12:28). And because of His humble obedience, God glorified Him (8:54).

These verses end with a quote from Psalm 2:7. We noted in Hebrews 1:5 that readers recognized this as a messianic prophecy in which God said, "You are My Son, today I have begotten You." Paul explained in Acts 13:33 that this was fulfilled when God "raised up Jesus." Christ was "Son" and "Priest" (Hebrew 5:5-6). How could Jewish Christians have considered leaving the better One for a sinful, human substitute? How can anyone today?

List some differences between Christ and earthly priests.

Priest and King (Hebrews 5:6)
6 As He also says in another place: "You are a priest forever according to the order of Melchizedek."

The writer now would emphasize Christ's superiority over earthly priests with an interesting comparison. He introduced an ancient high priest of whom readers had heard from the Scriptures, a man named

Melchizedek. He also quoted from Psalm 110:4, another text accepted as messianic. But readers did not fully understand its connection with Jesus. The writer would try to explain.

Jesus fulfilled a unique position as a priest after the order of Melchizedek. This priest and king of Salem lived in the days of Abraham and was superior to the Jewish forefather. Abraham was neither a priest nor a king. Not even Aaron held both positions. But Jesus was described in Scripture as both King and High Priest (Matthew 21:4; Hebrews 3:1). The writer had more to say about Melchizedek, but he stopped to discuss the unique preparation Jesus endured to become a better high priest. Read about Melchizedek in Genesis 14:18-20.

> *Made Perfect through Suffering (Hebrews 5:7-10)*
> **7** ... *who, in the days of His flesh, when He had offered up prayers and supplications, with vehement cries and tears to Him who was able to save Him from death, and was heard because of His godly fear,* **8** *though He was a Son, yet He learned obedience by the things which He suffered.* **9** *And having been perfected, He became the author of eternal salvation to all who obey Him,* **10** *called by God as High Priest "according to the order of Melchizedek."*

Unlike human priests, Jesus was sinless. However, to be better equipped for His priestly function, He had to go through a refinement process and learn perfect obedience. Of course, Jesus had always obeyed the Father, but accepting the cross was a challenge. His human side did not want to go through that agony. Russ Dudrey summarized,

> As the Gospels present Jesus' struggle in the Garden of Gethsemane, Jesus prayed there repeatedly ... 'Father, if it be possible let this cup pass from me'; that is, 'Father, I don't want to die, I don't want to die, I don't want to die.' Hebrews concludes that through facing squarely such struggles as Gethsemane and winning through to obedience, despite his own wishes to the contrary, Jesus became qualified as our High Priest.[66]

The experience began on the night before His crucifixion; three Gospels record it (Matthew 26:36-46; Mark 14:32-42; Luke 22:39-46). There, in Gethsemane, Jesus described His emotional state as "deeply distressed ... [and] exceedingly sorrowful, even to death" (Matthew 26:37-38). He prayed three times for deliverance from the cross: "If it is possible, let this cup pass from Me" (vv. 39, 42, 44). But He ended each petition with "Not as I will, but as You will" (vv. 39, 42). Because of His godly fear, "reverential awe, which implies a total submission to His Father," Jesus' prayers were answered.[67] He would submit to the cross, but God sent an angel to strengthen Him in His distress (Luke 22:43).

This perfection process was necessary so that Jesus could become the author of our salvation. We read this in Hebrews 2:10. The Greek term for "perfect" implies a maturity that comes only through trials and suffering (James 1:2-4). Pace clarified, "Obedience is never perfected until it is done without question. ... When we have completely obeyed, we are then made perfect, entire, and mature as saints."[68] We, too, must learn this kind of obedience. We cannot choose which commands to obey and ignore the rest. Eternal salvation is available only to those who obey Him (Hebrews 5:9).

The trials that perfect us form the crosses we must bear. As in the garden, God does not always take away trials, but He does provide strength to endure them. William Barclay commented, "Things happen to every one of us in this world that we cannot understand; it is then that faith is tried to its utmost limits; and at such a time it is sweetness to the soul that in Gethsemane Jesus went through that too. ... Every man has his private Gethsemane, and every man has to learn to say, 'Thy will be done.'" [69] Sisters, have you leaned on our High Priest through a private Gethsemane? Only a hardened heart can deny this sweetness to the soul.

Share a specific trial that produced spiritual maturity in your life.

These first verses of Hebrews 5 form an inspired picture of Jesus' high priesthood. They reveal His unique qualification as the merciful, faithful, and sinless One who both offered and constituted the perfect sacrifice for our sins. He did not seek honor for Himself, but was called by God. Paul beautifully summarized Jesus' perfection process and reward: "And being found in appearance as a man, He humbled Himself and became obedient to the point of death, even the death of the cross.

Therefore God also has highly exalted Him and given Him the name which is above every name" (Philippians 2:8-9). We are privileged to call Him our High Priest.

Describe the "perfect obedience" Jesus had to
learn and the reason for it. (See Hebrews 5:8-9.)

REBUKE FOR SPIRITUAL LAZINESS (HEBREWS 5:11-14)

Twice in chapter 5, the Hebrews writer referred to the ancient priest and king Melchizedek. He wanted to present more information about this man as a type and shadow of Christ, but it was hard for him to communicate. His readers lacked the spiritual maturity to understand. Pace noted, "The maturity that the writer desired for the Christians to whom he wrote was a capability to grasp and appreciate the exposition of truth on an advanced level. ... It is sad when men and women who have been Christians for years are found to be unaware of spiritual realities which should have great meaning, appeal, and power for them."[70]

Lack of Bible Study (Hebrews 5:11-12)
11 *... of whom we have much to say, and hard to explain, since you have become dull of hearing.* **12** *For though by this time you ought to be teachers, you need someone to teach you again the first principles of the oracles of God; and you have come to need milk and not solid food.*

The readers had neglected deep study of the Scriptures and were in a downward spiral toward drifting, doubting, and worse. So the writer began the third of five warnings in Hebrews:

- Do not *drift* from the Word—Hebrews 2:1-4 (neglect)
- Do not *doubt* the Word—Hebrews 3:7–4:13 (hard heart)
- **> Do not become *dull* toward the Word—Hebrews 5:11–6:20 (sluggishness)**
- Do not *despise* the Word—Hebrews 10:26-39 (willfulness)
- Do not *defy* the Word—Hebrews 12:25-29 (refusing to hear)

Lack of Bible study produces spiritual sluggishness. Does this describe you? It can happen to anyone. These readers had been washed and enlightened, had tasted the goodness of God's Word, and had once lived a consistent Christian lifestyle.[71] They may have lived in Jerusalem, the buckle of the ancient Bible belt where Peter and Paul had preached, but they had become mentally lazy (dull of hearing) and had actually regressed. Leon Morris and Donald Burdick noted that in the Christian life "one either moves forward or slips back. It is almost impossible to stand still."[72] Readers needed a rebuke for their condition. So the writer digressed from his discussion of Melchizedek and Christ's priesthood to write Hebrews 5:11-12.

No one likes to be called a baby. This humiliating metaphor surely got their attention. Perhaps the writer used reverse psychology, hoping they would "take the dare and be willing to jump in as he leaps into the theological depths."[73] The rebuke was not a pleasant task, but it was necessary to save their souls.

When we are baptized, we are spiritually born again (John 3:5). Then, like physical babies, we must grow (2 Peter 3:18). Peter exhorted new Christians, "As newborn babes, desire the sincere milk of the word, that you may grow thereby" (1 Peter 2:2). Milk provides nourishment for infants until they are able to digest solid food. In the same way, new converts must learn simple truths of God's Word before they can understand deeper concepts. They would choke on more complex and challenging theological material. But, in time, they must handle "meat."

These readers were spiritually immature. The Corinthian church had the same problem. Paul wrote to them, "And I, brethren, could not speak unto you as unto spiritual, but as unto carnal, as unto babes in Christ. I fed you with milk, not with meat; for ye were not yet able to bear it: nay, not even now are ye able" (1 Corinthians 3:1-2 ASV). We find other parallels of the child and the mature Christian in 1 Corinthians 2:6, 14:20, and Ephesians 4:13-14.

The Hebrew Christians needed to advance from spiritual childhood to maturity—that is, from milk to meat. In fact, enough time had passed that they should have already been teaching others. Each of us is to be ready always to give an answer concerning our hope (1 Peter 3:15). Although we may not teach formal Bible classes, we must share the gospel with others (Matthew 28:19-20; Mark 16:15-16). We are commanded to study, learn, grow, and teach. These readers were not growing, nor were they teaching.

In fact, it appears they were in a worse condition. They had become spiritually malnourished. We might compare them to the pitiful, starving toddlers living in third-world countries. No matter their age, new Christians must begin with liquid nourishment and move slowly to solid food. The original readers had neglected study and forgotten the simple "first principles" of God's Word. The writer said they needed to go back and relearn the basic elements of Christianity before moving on to deeper, meatier concepts.

---

*Discuss the importance of both types of
Bible classes and sermons: basic elements
and more advanced, complex principles.*

Sadly, some today believe that first principles are all we need. W. Jones observed,

> It is pitiful and painful to reflect upon the prevalence of spiritual obtuseness in our own age. How many Christians are perfectly content and self-satisfied having only the barest rudiments of Scripture truth! Some even pride themselves in holding "the truth," as though they had grasped and mastered all truth; and in their firm adherence to "the simple gospel," as though there were no profundities and sublimities in the gospel of Jesus Christ. We fear that the Bible is far more widely circulated than read, and far more extensively read than studied or understood.[74]

The prescription to invigorate tired churches and lethargic members is to give them meat! When Paul told Titus to preach "sound" (meaning "healthy") doctrine, he used the term *hugiaino*, which can be understood "in the sense that the truth produces spiritual well-being" (Titus 2:1).[75]

Paul told Titus to preach "sound" (meaning "healthy") doctrine or "truth that produces spiritual well-being."

Elementary biblical principles will sustain for a while, but to maintain vitality for a long period, we need depth and roots.[76] These readers were spiritually immature because they did not study. Sisters, how many of us can be diagnosed with this deficiency?

Need for Spiritual Maturity (Hebrews 5:13-14)
13 *For everyone who partakes only of milk is unskilled in the word of righteousness, for he is a babe.* **14** *But solid food belongs to those who are of full age, that is, those who by reason of use have their senses exercised to discern both good and evil.*

The process of development from childhood to adulthood requires going beyond drinking milk to eating solid food. Spiritually speaking, the Christian must move past first principles and go on to advanced truths. Peter explained a step-by-step process toward maturity in 2 Peter 1:57: "Giving all diligence, add to your faith virtue, to virtue knowledge, to knowledge self-control, to self-control perseverance, to perseverance godliness, to godliness brotherly kindness, and to brotherly kindness love." Knowledge is an important step in that process.

Lack of Bible knowledge keeps one immature and naive, unable to discern good from evil (Hebrews 5:13). Babies do not have the ability to discriminate between good and bad, and they often put harmful things in their mouths. People who do not know right from wrong are also in danger. Spiritual discernment is not inborn. It must be sharpened by two things: (1) right teaching, which comes by studying the word of righteousness, and (2) right reasoning, which comes by exercising the word in life's experiences. God's Word provides right teaching, but we must read, meditate, and study in order to understand and apply it (2 Timothy 2:15). Then, we must use this knowledge in everyday life. Paul said we must exercise ourselves spiritually (1 Timothy 4:7). The term translated "exercise" is from *gumnazo*, meaning "to train the body or mind."[77] Biblical study and practice will help us learn discernment between good and evil.

A good illustration is the way bank tellers learn to distinguish real money from counterfeit. They learn what authentic bills feel like by repetitive handling. There is no need to learn what counterfeit bills look and feel like. The tellers become so familiar with authentic bills that when they touch a counterfeit, they can easily tell the difference. In the same way, mature Christians know Scripture so well that when they hear false teaching, they know it is not truth. They can discern good and evil. Those who do not know God's Word are vulnerable to false teaching and, therefore, easily prone to drifting, doubting, and becoming dull of hearing.

The answer for a tired church and depressed members is spiritual meat or knowledge of the Scriptures. Drifting from the Word produces doubt of its inspiration and its ability to relate to modern circumstances. Those in this downward spiral become dull of hearing and will seek solutions outside of Scripture. By listening to other voices, their teaching and practices will no longer identify them as the Lord's church. Sisters, consider implementing a daily Bible reading schedule for yourself and members of your congregation.

SUMMARY AND LOOKING FORWARD TO THE NEXT CHAPTER

The Hebrews writer was concerned about his readers drifting, doubting, and becoming dull of hearing. Some admired the earthly splendor of the Jewish high priesthood, but Jesus fulfilled that role in a better way. He is the compassionate, sinless sacrificial Lamb, perfected by His obedience unto death on the cross and called by God as High Priest. His position is greater than Aaron's, for He was appointed according to the royal, priestly order of Melchizedek. Readers were too spiritually immature to understand this. Their lack of Bible study had produced an inability to comprehend complex truths of God's Word. Therefore, they failed in the natural progression to grow in and share the gospel.

How does a lack of Bible knowledge make one vulnerable to false teaching? Discuss ways to make time for study.

In Hebrews 6, the writer encouraged his readers to "press on to maturity" (v. 1 NASB). He explained how to grow spiritually through deep Bible study. He commended their love and good works and encouraged them to trust God's promises. Abraham was used as an example. If they wanted to enter God's rest, they needed to diligently work toward spiritual maturity. This would help them withstand persecution and persevere to the end.

CHAPTER 6

KEEP MOVING FORWARD
(HEBREWS 6)

In the opening scene of *Love Comes Softly*, Marty and her husband, Aaron, stopped their covered wagon to assess their progress. They had begun with high hopes, but drifting from the path had discouraged them. When they turned their eyes in the right direction, their hope was restored. Marty clasped Aaron's hand and was comforted by his promise that, "even if things get rough," her hope for a better life would be fulfilled. This gave her strength to keep moving forward.

Hope and promises inspire weary travelers. This was on the writer's mind as he wrote the words in Hebrews 6. After rebuking his readers for their spiritual laziness, he urged them to press on to perfection (v. 1), hope to the end (v. 11), and trust in God's promises (vv. 13-20). Hope in His promises enables us to keep moving on our journey to a better place. Thomas Long added,

> One must always be moving, and there are only two directions in which one can move: deeper or adrift. Either we keep growing, maturing, becoming more profound in our faith, or we are content to float lazily along the surface, unaware that the treacherous currents are pulling us more and more off course until we are hopelessly lost.[78]

To maintain hope and overcome obstacles, we must "press on unto perfection" (Hebrews 6:1 ASV). "Perfect" does not mean sinless; it means mature, full-grown, complete. Thompson clarified,

Maturity and "perfection" are both translations of the Greek *teleiotes*. The word, suggesting the idea of "completion," is extremely important for Hebrews. ... The word here suggests the opposite of "dull of hearing" in 5:12. The mature, according to 5:14, are the ones whose spiritual skills have been trained to accept "solid food" (i.e., deeper instruction) and to know good from evil. This maturity consists in going beyond elementary instruction, for the church can be redeemed from apostasy only when it grasps that Jesus as high priest (ch.7) is adequate for the needs of a persecuted church (10:32).[79]

Perfection as a high degree of spiritual maturity is possible. Paul declared in 1 Corinthians 2:6, "However, we speak wisdom among those who are mature." In Philippians 3:15, he wrote, "Therefore let us, as many as are mature, have this mind." Epaphras, a coworker with Paul, fervently prayed that the Colossians might "stand perfect and complete in all the will of God" (Colossians 4:12). Spiritual maturity comes with studying the meat of God's Word.

Define the term "perfection" according to Hebrews 6:1,
and discuss its possibility for Christians today.

Learning to handle or digest advanced theological material will help us become perfect in the sense discussed here. The Hebrews writer explained how.

Go Beyond Basic Principles (Hebrews 6:1-3)
1 *Therefore, leaving the discussion of the elementary principles of Christ, let us go on to perfection, not laying again the foundation of repentance from dead works and of faith toward God,* **2** *of the doctrine of baptisms, of laying on of hands, of resurrection of the dead, and of eternal judgment.* **3** *And this we will do if God permits.*

These Christians were stuck in the elementary principles of salvation. Of course, repetition is not bad. The basic teachings about Christ (milk) must be reviewed periodically. If not, each new generation will be in danger of drifting. But no one can build a house by focusing only on the foundation. We grow spiritually by learning higher principles (meat).

In Hebrews 6:1-3, the writer listed six basic concepts taught to Jewish converts. The word "therefore" connects the rebuke in Hebrews 5:11-14 with the encouragement in 6:1-8. *Because* they were spiritually immature and *because* they could not grow without learning deep biblical truths, they (*therefore*) needed to go beyond the basics and progress toward maturity. Six elementary concepts are listed here in pairs: two initial experiences, two symbolic expressions, and two future events.[80]

1. First-century believers learned about *faith in Jesus as God's Son* and *repentance from dead works* (sinful practices). Repentance means to change one's mind and actions with godly sorrow (Acts 2:38; Luke 13:3, 5).

2. The two symbolic practices in which Jewish converts were instructed were *baptisms* and *laying on of hands*. "Baptisms" is plural because early Christians were taught the differences between Jewish and pagan ceremonial washings, John's baptism, and baptism into Christ (John 3:25; Acts 19:1-5).[81] Laying on of hands, in that day, was associated with blessing, prayer, and the passing on of miraculous spiritual gifts. The latter ceased when the New Testament scriptures were complete (1 Corinthians 13:9-10).

3. The last pair involved truths about life after death: *resurrection of the dead* and *eternal judgment* (1 Corinthians 15:12-17; Matthew 25:31-46; Acts 17:30-31).

Basic principles are essential. Among the "basics" in Christianity are elements in the plan of salvation: hear, believe, repent, confess, and be baptized. Resurrection and judgment remain elementary principles. After learning these, we must progress to deeper, growth-producing concepts. Hebrews discusses several, such as our relationship with Christ as our High Priest and God's providence in our Christian journey.

Do you believe you have grown beyond the elementary principles in your spiritual knowledge? If not, what can you do to continue learning?

His involvement, even in our maturity process, is referenced in Hebrews 6:3: "And this we will do if God permits." In that day, it was common to say "if God wills" (cf. Acts 18:21).[82] We, too, should acknowledge God in our plans, both privately and publicly (cf. 1 Corinthians 16:7). If we desire spiritual growth, we need God's help, and He is able to help us take our study beyond the basics.

Discuss the importance of vocalizing the concept "if God wills."

The Point of No Return (Hebrews 6:4-6)

4 *For it is impossible for those who were once enlightened, and have tasted the heavenly gift, and have become partakers of the Holy Spirit,* **5** *and have tasted the good word of God and the powers of the age to come,* **6** *if they fall away, to renew them again to repentance, since they crucify again for themselves the Son of God, and put Him to an open shame.*

Hebrews 6:4-6 reveals the importance of staying on the better path, for if we leave, we may not be able to return. Without spiritual maturity, we will drift, doubt, become dull of hearing, and fall away. "Once saved, always saved" is not true.

Readers had been enlightened (brought to God's light), had been baptized, and had begun the Christian life (Ephesians 5:8). They had fully tasted (experienced) the heavenly gift of salvation (John 4:10); partaken of the Holy Spirit by allowing His work in their lives (7:37-39; Galatians 4:6); and enjoyed the blessings of the gospel (God's power for salvation in the Christian age, Romans 1:16). These converts had practiced Christianity with fervor (Hebrews 6:10), but by neglecting Bible study and worship, they began to backslide (drift, doubt, and become dull of hearing). So the writer gave them a stern warning about the state into which they were headed: full-blown apostasy (3:12; 10:26). From that state, "it is impossible ... to renew them again to repentance" (6:4-6).

Of course, Christians can repent of sin and be forgiven (1 John 1:9), but if they completely abandon Christ, they can reach a point of no return. Lightfoot explained, "[This is] because he has traveled the road of falling and renewal so much that for him the whole matter is a trifle. His heart has turned cold, his life listless, and his condition is such that he can no longer turn from sin. It is impossible for him to be saved because he is *incapable* of turning to God."[83] Sisters, do you know Christians who keep one foot in the world and one in the church, going back and forth between the two until they leave the Lord altogether? In 2 Peter 2:20-22, Peter described these apostates in a graphic manner:

> For if, after they have escaped the pollutions of the world through the knowledge of the Lord and Savior Jesus Christ, they are again entangled in them and overcome, the latter end is worse for them than the beginning. For it would have been better for them not to have known the way of righteousness, than having known it, to turn from the holy commandment delivered to them. But it has happened to them according to the true proverb: "A dog returns to his own vomit," and, "a sow, having washed, to her wallowing in the mire."

What a sickening sight! So it is with souls who abandon the faith, harden their hearts, and refuse to repent. To make matters worse, their negative example hurts the cause of Christ. An apostate Christian stands before the world as a disillusioned convert, "like a friend turned traitor."[84] They disgrace Christ even more than unbelievers because they figuratively crucify Him a second time. One commentator stated that "in heart and mind they make themselves one with those who put him to death."[85] We must help those headed in this wrong direction!

What is meant in Hebrews 6:4-6 when it says
that it is impossible for those who have experienced
and fallen away from Christianity to repent?

Blessings and Curses (Hebrews 6:7-8)
7 *For the earth which drinks in the rain that often comes upon it, and bears herbs useful for those by whom it is cultivated, receives blessing from God;* **8** *but if it bears thorns and briars, it is rejected and near to being cursed, whose end is to be burned.*

Next, the writer presented an illustration similar to the parable of the soils. It shows two types of vegetation from land nourished by God.

God sends rain on the just and the unjust (Matthew 5:45), on good soil and bad. When soil yields good fruit, it is blessed to yield more. But if it bears thorns, it is useless, is cursed, and must be destroyed. Similarly, Christians who involve themselves in Bible study, service, and other spiritual growth–producing activities benefit themselves and others and bring glory to God. They are blessed (Psalm 1:1-2; Matthew 25:34-36). But those who experience salvation and blessings in Christianity and then reject it are cursed. In the natural order of God's earthly and spiritual kingdom, elements that do not produce fruit will suffer a tragic end (John 15:2, 5-6).

After this warning, the writer gave readers words of comfort and hope. He expressed his confidence in them and assured them that God knew their love and good works. He reminded them of future rewards of hope and faith in His promises.

Encouraging Words (Hebrews 6:9-12)
9 *But, beloved, we are confident of better things concerning you, yes, things that accompany salvation, though we speak in this manner.* **10** *For God is not unjust to forget your work and labor of love which you have shown toward His name, in that you have ministered to the saints, and do minister.* **11** *And we desire that each one of you show the same diligence to the full assurance of hope until the end,* **12** *that you do not become sluggish, but imitate those who through faith and patience inherit the promises.*

The writer loved his readers and fully expected them to revive from their sluggishness. Their good works were a positive sign that they could regain their desire to grow and bear fruit.

Despite their inadequacies, the writer would not give up on them. Though faith and hope had waned, their ministry to saints had not (Hebrews 10:33-34). The term "minister" (from which the word "deacon" comes) means "wait on someone," "serve" to meet needs.[86] The service these Christians rendered, especially to the household of faith, revealed their love (1 John 3:16-18; 4:20-21). The writer reciprocated this feeling and called them "beloved" (Hebrews 6:9). Note how Paul used this same term in his letter to the Thessalonians:

> We give thanks to God always for you all, making mention of you in our prayers, remembering without ceasing your work of faith, labor of love, and patience of hope in our Lord Jesus Christ in the sight of our God and Father, knowing, beloved brethren, your election by God. (1 Thessalonians 1:2-4)

Note that Paul commended the Thessalonians' labor of love, works of faith, and patience of hope. Often in Scripture we find faith, hope, and love listed together as traits of strong Christians (1 Corinthians 13:13). The Hebrews readers exhibited love, but lacked faith and hope (Hebrews 6:10-12). They were diligent in good works, but these alone would not save. They had continued their actions of ministry, but not their study of the Word. Hebrews 6:12, just as 5:11, describes them as "sluggish."

How can a group lacking faith and hope but rich in love still fall away from Christ? Is your congregation strong in all three elements? How about you?

The writer implored them to be diligent—the opposite of sluggish. He assured them that the God of justice sees and rewards Christian service (Hebrews 6:10; 11:6). But in order to inherit His promises, they needed to show "full assurance of hope until the end" (6:11). And they were to imitate others who had persevered and received their reward. Pace observed,

> The faithful dead have already entered into life and have inherited God's promises. This was true of Lazarus when he died (Lk.16:22, 25) and of Jesus, who was "made alive" in the spirit at His death (1 Pet.3:18). If the readers continued to copy the faithful who had gone before them, they would obtain the same reward as a fulfillment of God's promises. They would receive this reward through faith and patient endurance, and the same is true for us. We must not be overwhelmed by the length of time or the weight of the burdens along the way, for they are "light" compared to the "weight" of our reward in glory (2 Cor. 4:17,18).[87]

Having godly examples can inspire hope and confidence. The last section of Hebrews 6 focuses on a particular godly model from the Jews' own ancestry: Abraham. Abraham lived by faith in God's promises. In fact, despite obstacles in his long life journey, he persevered and was able to see early fulfillment of his hope.

HOPE IN GOD'S PROMISES (HEBREWS 6:13-20)

Hope can inspire confidence and revive discouraged Christians. Thompson explained,

> A tired church cannot live without hope. ... Hebrews resonates with hope because weary people need to know that their pilgrimage is directed toward a goal. We can learn much from Hebrews. We learn with the original readers to give up false hopes which turn out to be mirages. We reaffirm the one hope that nourishes our lives and motivates us to keep the faith.[88]

A tired church cannot live without hope. This was true in the first century and remains true today. Sisters, are you able to sing these words with confidence: "My hope is built on nothing less than Jesus' blood and righteousness"? Hebrews 6:13-20 encourages renewed hope in Jesus' power to save; this hope is based on God's promises. As a model of doubt, the writer had reviewed the Israelites' failure to enter the Promised Land (Hebrews 3:5–4:11). Now, he presented a model of patient trust: the revered patriarch of the Hebrew nation, Abraham.

Name a Christian woman you know who models
faith and hope. How does her example encourage you?

Promises Fulfilled (Hebrews 6:13-18)
13 *For when God made a promise to Abraham, because He could swear by no one greater, He swore by Himself,* **14** *saying, "Surely blessing I will bless you, and multiplying I will multiply you."* **15** *And so, after he had patiently endured, he obtained the promise.* **16** *For men indeed swear by the greater, and an oath for confirmation is for them an end of all dispute.* **17** *Thus God, determining to show more abundantly to the heirs of promise the immutability of His counsel, confirmed it by an oath,* **18** *that by*

two immutable things, in which it is impossible for God to lie, we might
have strong consolation, who have fled for refuge to lay hold of the hope
set before us.

In Genesis, God promised to give Abraham a great land, a great nation, a great name, and a great blessing for all nations through his seed
(12:1-7). Abraham believed and followed God to the Promised Land.
He patiently waited twenty-five years for Isaac (v. 4; 21:5) and sixty
more years for grandchildren (25:26). Through eyes of faith, he also
saw the blessing for all nations through the future Messiah (John 8:56).
Paul wrote of Abraham, he "believed God, and it was accounted to him
for righteousness" (Galatians 3:6). The Hebrews writer reviewed God's
promise to Abraham, emphasizing the fact that God swore an oath.

Readers were familiar with this oath in Genesis 22:1-18. God made
it just after Abraham passed his famous test of faith on Mount Mori-
ah. Review this narrative to better grasp its significance here. God had
commanded Abraham to offer Isaac as a sacrifice. Abraham showed
confidence and hope that God would raise up his son and fulfill His
promises. As he lifted the knife, God stopped his hand, reiterated the
covenant, and confirmed His promise with an oath.

What made Abraham an example of faith and hope?
What do you love most, and could you give it up to obey God?

Ancient covenants were considered legally guaranteed when parties
gave a sworn promise. Sealing it with an oath settled a matter so that
nothing could contradict it. Parties also swore by the name of someone
superior to themselves, someone who could punish if they broke their
promise. This is practiced today when a court witness places a hand on
the Bible and swears to tell the truth, the whole truth, and nothing but
the truth "so help me God." There is a consequence to broken oaths.
But God does not break His promises.

No one is greater than God, so when He made a promise, He guaranteed it by His own existence (Hebrews 6:13). But why would God, who

cannot lie, need to swear an oath? He did it to strengthen man's confidence in the promise. Lightfoot suggested that God added the oath to "show more convincingly ... the unchangeable character of his purpose" for Abraham and "all his spiritual descendants (Christians) as well (Gal.3:7)."[89] It is sad that we humans cannot just take God at His word.

God did fulfill His promise of a blessing for all nations; it was fulfilled through His Son. Therefore, Christians, as Abraham's spiritual descendants, share this hope. The Hebrews readers needed encouragement to be patient in this hope. We, as heirs according to this promise, also must patiently endure life's trials as we wait (Galatians 3:29; Romans 4:11-13). Abraham's hope required years of patient waiting, and after his death, he received fulfillment of the final covenant God made with him (Matthew 8:11). If we persevere to the end, we will too.

Just as ancient law required two witnesses to establish a fact (Deuteronomy 17:6), the Hebrews writer further confirmed God's promise with two witnesses. These were (1) God's immutable counsel and (2) His oath (Hebrews 6:17). "Immutable" ("unchangeable," KJV) means "unable to be changed."[90] Lenski noted, "Any of his readers who would turn away from Christ and revert to Judaism would thereby charge God with a double lie: that his promise does not mean what it says; that his oath is perjury."[91]

Name some of God's promises that
give you hope in your Christian journey.

This letter offered encouragement to persevere through hope in God's steadfast promises. We can trust God to keep His promises. They are our refuge, our place to flee in trying circumstances. Dear sisters, have you leaned on God's promises as you patiently wait?

A Sure Hope (Hebrews 6:19-20)
19 *This hope we have as an anchor of the soul, both sure and steadfast, and which enters the Presence behind the veil,* **20** *where the forerunner*

has entered for us, even Jesus, having become High Priest forever according to the order of Melchizedek.

Because God keeps His promises, Christians have a sure hope of ending our journey in that better place. This sure and steadfast hope is described as "an anchor of the soul."

Some of our hymns use the biblical metaphor of an anchor. One includes this chorus by Priscilla J. Owens: "We have an anchor that keeps the soul steadfast and sure while the billows roll, fastened to the Rock which cannot move, grounded firm and deep in the Savior's love." An anchor provides a stabilizing force to help a ship stay secure and firm, "undisturbed by outward influences," so that sailors have no worry of drifting.[92] Our confidence in God's promises and hope of heaven keep us anchored in Christianity. Being anchored keeps us from drifting and falling into apostasy.

Discuss the metaphor "anchor of the soul"
as it describes our hope in Christ.

The Hebrews writer returned to his discussion of Christ's priesthood. Readers understood that, in Judaism, only the high priest had access to God's presence. He entered the Most Holy Place once a year to offer the atoning sacrifice for their sins. But Jesus offered Himself as the final and sufficient sacrifice. The veil was literally torn in two as He figuratively entered that sacred area and opened it up for us. This is stated explicitly in Hebrews 9:12: "Not with the blood of goats and calves, but with His own blood He entered the Most Holy Place once for all, having obtained eternal redemption."

Our hope allows us to enter God's presence in prayer and have an expectation of doing so in heaven. This cannot be found in any other religion (Acts 4:12). The Old Testament high priests paled in comparison to our High Priest, Jesus Christ. He leads us in our journey to that better place.

SUMMARY AND LOOKING FORWARD TO THE NEXT CHAPTER

The Hebrews writer was concerned about his readers' spiritual lethargy. He directed them to press on to perfection, to diligently study the deep truths of God's Word, and to apply them to life. Anyone who drifts, doubts, becomes dull of hearing, and then falls away can reach a point of no return. The writer commended the readers' love and service, but urged increased faith and hope. He held up Abraham as an example of hope and patience for fulfillment of God's promises. We, as his spiritual descendants, share this hope.

The writer had begun a discussion of Christ's high priesthood in Hebrews 5, but digressed for a rebuke and an encouraging word about hope in God's promises. He ended Hebrews 6 with a reference to Jesus as our "High Priest forever according to the order of Melchizedek" (v. 20). In Hebrews 7, he returned to this topic for an in-depth discussion.

CHAPTER 7

FOLLOW THE GUIDE
(HEBREWS 7)

E very successful journey requires a wise and experienced leader. Imprudent guides make poor decisions. Edward John Smith, captain of the *Titanic*, is remembered for his failure. But Captain Meriwether Lewis and 2nd Lieutenant William Clark were memorialized for discovering a route across the American West. Everyone values the leader who reaches the goal. In the Christian pilgrimage, we have the perfect guide in Jesus.

Sadly, some Jewish converts had forgotten Christ's unique qualifications. He was the compassionate, sinless sacrifice, perfected by obedience in His death on the cross and called by God as High Priest. His position was greater than even Aaron's, for He was appointed according to the royal, priestly order of Melchizedek. The Jews knew David spoke of this order as a type and shadow of the Messiah (Psalm 110:4), but they had not clearly connected it with Jesus. The Hebrews writer had begun to explain, but his readers were too immature to understand. They were spiritually stagnant. So he digressed from his discussion to rebuke and encourage them to greater maturity and hope in God's promises.

Now, in the central part of the letter (Hebrews 7:1–10:18), his focus returned to Christ's priesthood. This section opens with a description of Melchizedek and his superiority over both Abraham and the Levitical priesthood. (All Jewish priests were descendants of Levi, the great-grandson of Abraham).

Hebrews 7 can be divided into three evidences based on Old Testament texts:

1. Melchizedek's priesthood was greater than Aaron's (vv. 1-10).
2. God promised a new Melchizedek-like priesthood (vv. 11-17).
3. Christ's priesthood is superior (vv. 18-28).[93]

MELCHIZEDEK'S SUPERIOR PRIESTHOOD (HEBREWS 7:1-10)

Knowing that the original letter was written without chapter and verse divisions, we can easily connect "Jesus, having become High Priest forever according to the order of Melchizedek" at the end of Hebrews 6 with "this Melchizedek ... [who] remains a priest continually" (7:1-3). The latter three verses describe the Old Testament priest/king as a type and shadow of our Lord.

Timeless Priest and King of Salem (Hebrews 7:1-3)
1 *For this Melchizedek, king of Salem, priest of the Most High God, who met Abraham returning from the slaughter of the kings and blessed him,* **2** *to whom also Abraham gave a tenth part of all, first being translated "king of righteousness," and then also king of Salem, meaning "king of peace,"* **3** *without father, without mother, without genealogy, having neither beginning of days nor end of life, but made like the Son of God, remains a priest continually.*

In Hebrews 7:1-2, the writer summarized the Old Testament account in which Melchizedek blessed Abraham and accepted a tithe from him (Genesis 14:18-20). Then, to show this king/priest as a shadow of Jesus, he translated Melchizedek's titles, noted the absence of ancestry records, and compared his continual priesthood to that of God's Son.

First, Melchizedek's honored position was noted in the translation of his titles. His name in Hebrew means "king of righteousness," and the phrase "king of Salem" means "king of peace" (Hebrews 7:2). Jewish readers likely recognized these terms from Old Testament messianic prophecies (Isaiah 9:6-7; Jeremiah 23:5; Zechariah 6:12-13; 9:9, 10). These titles show the connection between priest/king Melchizedek and Priest/King Jesus.

Second, the writer obscured Melchizedek's birth, death, parentage, and posterity. Scripture generally gives an ancestry of renowned characters, usually naming their fathers, and the Jews were meticulous about keeping genealogical records (Ezra 2:62). Melchizedek was human, so he did have a family. But the absence of names here implies that his priesthood had no predecessors or successors, symbolizing the timeless priesthood of Christ.

Can you see the connection between Christ and Melchizedek? It helps us better understand the prophecy God gave through David: "You are a priest forever according to the order of Melchizedek" (Psalm 110:4). It was important for the spiritually dull readers to see Jesus as the fulfillment of the Melchizedek prophecy.

These Jewish converts revered their ancestor, Abraham, and the Levitical priesthood. This may have played a role in the inclination to return to Judaism. If the writer could show evidence that Melchizedek (a shadow of Christ) was greater than this Patriarch and his priestly descendants, it would prove Jesus' superiority over them also. Lenski wrote,

> The readers, former Jews who were now thinking of returning to Judaism, are here confronted with their great forefather Abraham and are shown how he accepted the royal priest Melchizedek long before Levi and Aaron were born and the Aaronitic high priesthood came into existence. The readers want to be true sons of Abraham, yea, are thinking of returning to Judaism for that very reason. Well, let them look at Abraham and at the one priest to whom Abraham bowed. Let them consider what God said through David regarding this royal priest and regarding the Messiah-Christ who is typified by Melchizedek.[94]

How was Melchizedek a type and shadow of Christ?

Greater than Abraham and His Descendants (Hebrews 7:4-10)
4 Now consider how great this man was, to whom even the patriarch Abraham gave a tenth of the spoils. 5 And indeed those who are of the sons of Levi, who receive the priesthood, have a commandment to receive tithes from the people according to the law, that is, from their brethren, though they have come from the loins of Abraham; 6 but he whose genealogy is not derived from them received tithes from Abraham and blessed him who had the promises. 7 Now beyond all contradiction the lesser is blessed by

the better. 8 Here mortal men receive tithes, but there he receives them, of whom it is witnessed that he lives. 9 Even Levi, who receives tithes, paid tithes through Abraham, so to speak, 10 for he was still in the loins of his father when Melchizedek met him.

The writer would now explain some difficult concepts. He stated earlier that these were hard to communicate. Sisters, if you find them challenging, just hang in there. Your eyes will be opened to some great biblical truths. The writer wanted to show Jesus as a "High Priest forever according to the order of Melchizedek" (Hebrews 6:20), so he used a method of biblical interpretation called *midrash*, which is a discussion of a scripture text to make application for readers.[95] From Genesis 14:18-20, he explained that Melchizedek was greater than Abraham. Melchizedek was a type of Christ; therefore, Christ is greater than Abraham.

Two events in this text give evidence that Melchizedek was greater than Abraham: (1) Abraham gave a tithe to Melchizedek, and (2) Melchizedek blessed Abraham. Readers knew the principles of religious superiority: priests received tithes from the Jewish populace (and not the other way around). And it is undeniable that the lesser man receives blessings from the greater (Hebrews 7:7).[96] So receiving a tithe and giving a blessing showed Melchizedek's superiority.

ABRAHAM'S TITHE (HEBREWS 7:4-8)

Jews knew all about tithing. The Law of Moses required it (Leviticus 27:30, 32). The people paid a tenth of their income to the Levites, and the Levites gave ten percent of these tithes to the priests (Numbers 18:24, 26, 28). Only Levites received tithes and only from their brethren. In contrast, Melchizedek could rightfully take tithes from all worshipers of God.[97] He served as priest before the Law of Moses was established.

Can you name some God-ordained priests before Aaron's appointment? See Genesis 14:18-20 and Exodus 3:1.

If Melchizedek had lived under the Law of Moses, he could not have been a priest, for non-Levites were disqualified (Nehemiah 7:63-64). But he was appointed before the time of Levitical priests. Hebrews 7:6 proclaims that his "genealogy is not derived from them." He was a priest *not* from the tribe of Levi. Similarly, Jesus was not from Levi. He descended from Levi's brother Judah. Yet He was the God-appointed priest that annulled the Levitical priesthood. This reality should help readers better understand and accept Jesus' priestly qualifications.

LEVI'S TITHE THROUGH ABRAHAM (HEBREWS 7:9-10)

Hebrews 7:9-10 reveals that Levi paid tithes to Melchizedek through Abraham. How can an unborn person pay tithes? The writer asserted that this was done "so to speak, for he was still in the loins of his father when Melchizedek met him" (Hebrews 7:9). "Loins" was a Hebrew term for the reproductive area of the body. Abraham's tithe symbolized a gift from yet-to-be-born Levi and all his future descendants. In Hebrew thought, this concept is called "federal representation" or "corporate personality," in which the individual represents the group (Romans 5:12; 1 Corinthians 15:22).[98]

Therefore, this tithe shows Melchizedek's superiority over yet-to-be-born Levi as an individual and over the yet-to-be-established Levitical priesthood as a group. Coffman declared, "The fact, therefore, of Abraham's taking a tithe of the chief spoils and paying them to Melchizedek, priest of God Most High, clearly made any priesthood developed through the descendants of Abraham to be subordinate to that of Melchizedek."[99] Morris summarized,

> The patriarch gave up a tenth of the spoils, thus implicitly acknowledging the superior place of Melchizedek. And Melchizedek proceeded to bless Abraham, accepting the implied superiority. The situation is clear to all parties. There is no need to spell it out. And the author is simply drawing attention to what the narrative clearly implies when he brings out the superior status of Melchizedek. Even when Abraham is seen as the one "who had the promises," Melchizedek is superior.[100]

If all Levitical priests were inferior to Melchizedek and Melchizedek was a type of Christ, then all Levitical priests were inferior to Christ. This was an important concept for Jewish Christians to comprehend and accept. Jesus is King and High Priest in the new and better covenant.

How did Abraham's tithe show that Melchizedek was greater than Levi and his priestly descendants?

Melchizedek-Like Priesthood (Hebrews 7:11-17)
11 *Therefore, if perfection were through the Levitical priesthood (for under it the people received the law), what further need was there that another priest should rise according to the order of Melchizedek, and not be called according to the order of Aaron?* **12** *For the priesthood being changed, of necessity there is also a change of the law.* **13** *For He of whom these things are spoken belongs to another tribe, from which no man has officiated at the altar.* **14** *For it is evident that our Lord arose from Judah, of which tribe Moses spoke nothing concerning priesthood.* **15** *And it is yet far more evident if, in the likeness of Melchizedek, there arises another priest* **16** *who has come, not according to the law of a fleshly commandment, but according to the power of an endless life.* **17** *For He testifies: "You are a priest forever according to the order of Melchizedek."*

The writer now emphasized the central message of his letter: "Only the religion of Christ brings men to God."[101] Judaism could not do this. It was imperfect and insufficient (Galatians 3:21, 24). God planned for a better covenant with a better Melchizedek-like priest. This is explained in Hebrews 7:11-17.

Some readers believed they could be saved under Judaism. But the Law of Moses was inadequate. The statement within the parentheses in Hebrews 7:11 shows that Israel's laws were based on the priesthood/sacrificial system. It was a system described as weak because of the people (Romans 8:3). Therefore, God's oath to send a new priest was significant. A change in the priesthood necessitated a change in the Law.[102]

That is exactly what Jesus did. In His Sermon on the Mount, He explained that He came not to destroy the Law, but to fulfill it. He quoted Old Law commandments and then stated, "But I say to you ... ." Jesus fulfilled those laws and stressed a deeper, heart-based element. God established the Old Law to deal with sin "till the Seed should come" (Galatians 3:19). Jesus was that promised Seed (Acts 13:22-23).

Trace the prophecy and fulfillment of Christ as the "Seed" using Genesis 3:15; 12:2-3; John 7:42; Acts 13:22-23; and Galatians 3:19.

The blood of bulls and goats could not take away sin, so God promised a transfer of priesthood from the Levites to one high priest "according to the order of Melchizedek" (Psalm 110:4). This new priest would arise from outside the Levites. The writer stated that "it is evident" (from their meticulous genealogical records) that Jesus came through the lineage of Judah, whose descendants never officiated at the altar (Hebrews 7:14). And it was "far more evident" that the new priest would come, like Melchizedek, not through the fleshly commandment (of human succession) but "according to the power of an endless life" (v. 16). God testified, "You are a priest forever" (v. 17).

THE BETTER PRIESTHOOD OF CHRIST (HEBREWS 7:18-28)

In Hebrews 7, the writer presented some deep and important truths for his readers to digest. His message was that only the religion of Christ brings men to God. As evidence, he made four contrasts between the old Jewish system and Christ's better priesthood: (1) this new priesthood brought "a better hope, through which we draw near to God" (v. 19); (2) God instituted it with an oath (v. 20); (3) the new Priest was eternal (v. 23); and (4) He had a pure and spotless character (v. 26). The earthly priests of Judaism paled in comparison to Jesus Christ.

A Better Hope (Hebrews 7:18-19)
18 *For on the one hand there is an annulling [setting aside[103]] of the former commandment because of its weakness and unprofitableness,* **19** *for the law made nothing perfect; on the other hand, there is the bringing in of a better hope, through which we draw near to God.*

The first contrast is that Christ's priesthood offers a better hope. What is this better hope? It is the blood of Jesus. It is better because it actually takes away sins (Hebrews 2:17; 1 John 1:7). Its power reached backward to enable the blood offered by the Levites to take away sin also. [104] What a difference! To trust in the Jewish faith for salvation was a delusion. Only the religion of Christ brings men to God.

Appointed with God's Oath (Hebrews 7:20-22)
20 *And inasmuch as He was not made priest without an oath* **21** *(for they have become priests without an oath, but He with an oath by Him who said to Him: "The LORD has sworn and will not relent, 'You are a priest forever according to the order of Melchizedek'"),* **22** *by so much more Jesus has become a surety of a better covenant.*

The second contrast is that God instituted Christ's priesthood with an oath. Hebrews 7:20-22 forms one long sentence, distinguishing Christ's better priesthood from the old order.

God never made an oath concerning the Levitical priests. But as we saw in Hebrews 6:16-17, He swore an oath for the Melchizedek-like appointee. In Psalm 110:4, David recorded not only the fact that God made an oath, but that He would never change His mind. Jesus Christ is a priest forever, not according to the Levitical system but according to the order of Melchizedek.

God's oath is His promise. But due to humanity's lack of faith, Jesus became the surety, or guarantor, of this covenant. "Surety" is defined as "one who pledges his name, property, or influence that a promise shall be fulfilled,"[105] and a "guarantor" is one who stands "good for a debt or the person who in a legal action might give bail for a prisoner."[106] Christians have double insurance for salvation! This provides encouragement to those struggling with faith in their journey to a better place.

Why did God offer double insurance for salvation to humans?
How did Jesus fulfill His pledge as guarantor?

An Eternal Priesthood (Hebrews 7:23-25)
23 *Also there were many priests, because they were prevented by death from continuing.* **24** *But He, because He continues forever, has an un-*

*changeable priesthood. 25 Therefore He is also able to save to the utter-
most those who come to God through Him, since He always lives to make
intercession for them.*

Readers knew the reality of this third contrast. When each human
high priest died, a successor was appointed. But Christ's is an unchangeable priesthood.

Josephus recorded eighty-three priests from Aaron to the fall of the
Jerusalem Temple in A.D. 70.[107] Perhaps readers had witnessed a funer-
al and/or an induction. They may have seen the last Jewish high priest,
Phannias, going about his sacrificial duties in the temple.

These verses assured readers that Jesus was superior. His unchangeable priesthood would continue to meet their needs "to the uttermost"
(completely). From His heavenly seat at God's right hand, Jesus made
intercession for His people. Milligan described this intercession as

> all that Christ is now doing for the justification, sanctification, and
> redemption of his people. Seated, as he is, on the right hand of the
> Father, and clothed with omnipotent power and authority, he is ever
> ready to plead for those who have been cleansed by his blood, ever
> ready to defend them against all the assaults of their enemies, and, in
> a word, ever ready to make all things work together for their good.[108]

What a comfort! Think about it, sisters. Why put trust in earthly
priests (or anyone else) when God's Son offers empathy, understanding, and true salvation?

Discuss our blessings from Christ's heavenly ministry today.

Pure and Spotless Character (Hebrews 7:26-28)
*26 For such a High Priest was fitting for us, who is holy, harmless, un-
defiled, separate from sinners, and has become higher than the heavens;
27 who does not need daily, as those high priests, to offer up sacrifices,
first for His own sins and then for the people's, for this He did once for all
when He offered up Himself. 28 For the law appoints as high priests men
who have weakness, but the word of the oath, which came after the law,
appoints the Son who has been perfected forever.*

The final verses of this chapter contrast the character of Christ and Jewish priests. The Law of Moses required that Levitical priests be without physical blemish (Leviticus 21:16-23). Yet readers knew that some had inner flaws revealed in outward corruption. In contrast, Jesus had a pure and spotless character. Five specific traits distinguished Him from earthly priests and qualified Him to be our great High Priest:

1. He is *holy*, just as God is holy (Mark 1:24; Leviticus 11:44).
2. He is *harmless*. Jesus loves us. While on earth, He went about doing good, and He continues this generosity by interceding in heaven (Acts 10:38; Romans 8:34).
3. He is *undefiled*. Blemished earthly priests and sacrifices were disqualified. Jesus fulfilled both roles because he was sinless (Hebrews 4:15).
4. He is *separate from sinners*. He is distinguished in character and is living in heaven (Hebrews 1:3).
5. He is *higher than the heavens*. He lives and serves at the right hand of God (Ephesians 4:10).

Hebrews 7:26-28 presents a summary of Jesus' superiority over the Jewish priests. Human priests sinned and needed to justify themselves through offerings before they could do so for the people. This was a daily ritual. In contrast, Jesus lived a sinless human life and was, therefore, qualified to be the perfect High Priest. He was also qualified to be the perfect, unblemished, once-for-all sacrifice. He offered Himself as a permanent propitiation for our sins. Lenski concluded, "What a fatal mistake, then, for the readers to think of forsaking 'such a High Priest' and turning back to Judaism, to the Levitical priests whose function had long been superseded as God himself declares in his sworn statement (v.20-22, 28)."[109]

How was Jesus more qualified to be a priest than any human?

SUMMARY AND LOOKING FORWARD TO THE NEXT CHAPTER

Through messianic prophecy, God promised a new High Priest "according to the order of Melchizedek." Both are described as timeless priests and kings, without genealogy, outside of Levi's lineage, and greater than Abraham and his priestly descendants. The Law of Moses was insufficient to remit sins, for only the religion of Christ brings men to God. This holy, unblemished Lamb came to earth and suffered as a human in order to be perfected and fitted for priestly service. He is holy, harmless, undefiled, separate from sinners, and higher than the heavens. Hebrews 8 opens with the fact that "we have such a High Priest!" And He established a new covenant, better than the inadequate Law of Moses. This new covenant will unite God's people, put His laws in their hearts, and forgive their sins.

CHAPTER 8

TURN RIGHT AT THE FORK
(HEBREWS 8)

I t must have been difficult and exciting for pioneers to climb into covered wagons, let go of the past, and look with anticipation to a better future. Consider the great trust they had in their guides. Good leaders kept up-to-date on weather conditions, hostile territories, and changes in terrain. Sometimes, they came upon an unexpected obstacle in their old path or a fork in the road, and they wisely made the right choice. Travelers, too, had to make a decision whether to remain on the faulty path or follow their experienced leader in the better way.

Hebrews is a reminder that Jesus is our better guide to heaven. He is the "trailblazer," who gave us a well-marked, though sometimes rocky, path to our better, eternal destination.[110] His gospel, when presented to Jews, became a fork in the road. They had to make a decision whether to remain on the faulty path or follow the Lord in the better way.

Not all viewed Christ's priesthood as the more excellent ministry. In the last few verses of Hebrews 7, the writer recapped God's oath to appoint One who was holy and sinless. In Hebrews 8:1, he proclaimed, "We have such a High Priest!" This chapter lies in the middle of the central part of the letter (7:1–10:18), showing Christ as the better High Priest and Mediator of a better covenant than the Law of Moses. Roger Omanson wrote,

> The dominant theme of this section, which brings the theological argument of the first seven chapters to its climax, is that in Jesus Christ we have a covenant superior to the one which God had established

with the people of Israel at Sinai. ... Throughout the letter the author informs his readers that they can find strength for living the Christian life by recognizing that the reality of God does not lie beyond them, out of their reach. So he writes, "We have a great high priest ..." (4:14); "We have confidence to enter the sanctuary ..." (10:19); "We have an altar ..." (13:10); "We have a clear conscience ..." (13:18). Now in 8:1 he declares, "We have such a high priest." It is not something potential or possible; it is a present reality.[111]

Jesus is our guide on the salvation trail to heaven. When the Jewish readers came to their fork in the road, they chose to turn right. Hebrews 8 presents significant differences between Judaism and Christianity. This will help us better understand the purpose of the Law of Moses and appreciate the Christian religion that replaced it.

The Main Point (Hebrews 8:1-2)

1 *Now this is the main point of the things we are saying: We have such a High Priest, who is seated at the right hand of the throne of the Majesty in the heavens,* **2** *a Minister of the sanctuary and of the true tabernacle which the Lord erected, and not man.*

Hebrews 8:1 presents the main point: Jesus alone is qualified to serve as our leader and guide. He is our great High Priest.

From His heavenly position, only Jesus can lead us on our journey to that better place. It should have been obvious to readers that mortal priests were just that: mortal. When each died, he was replaced. The old religious system was temporary. Milligan observed,

> As a religious Institution, it was, as we have seen, abolished when Christ was crucified. He then took it out of the way, nailing it to his cross (Col. 2:14). And as a civil Institution it continued for only about seven years after the writing of this Epistle. God then took it entirely out of the way, forever abolishing at the same time the whole Tabernacle service in order to stay more effectually the hand of persecution, and correct the extreme judaizing tendencies that were then threatening to corrupt the simplicity of the Gospel, especially throughout Palestine.[112]

Judaism was never intended to be permanent. God designed the Jewish system of earthly priests, animal sacrifices, and temple worship as a means to bring humanity to Christ. Read Galatians 3:24 and 4:4. At just the right time, He replaced it with a better system: Christianity. Jesus became the better High Priest. Human priests *stood* (Hebrews 10:11); Jesus majestically *sits* (v. 12). After becoming the once-for-all, perfect sacrifice, Jesus replaced human priests and their daily sacrifices. He ministers in a better temple. Interestingly, the Greek term for "minister" in Hebrews 8:2 is not *diakonos* ("one who serves," as in Matthew 23:11 and Mark 9:35), but *leitourgos*, "a public officer of high rank" or "a priestly minister" (Romans 13:6; 15:16; Philippians 2:25).[113]

The meaning of the Greek term "minister" in Hebrews 8:2 is not "one who serves" but "a public officer of high rank" or "a priestly minister."

Jesus is "a Minister of the sanctuary and of the true tabernacle." Commentators agree that, here, the terms "sanctuary" and "tabernacle" represent heavenly entities. The writer would now compare ministry in the physical holy place to that in the spiritual.

What is the main point of the Hebrews letter,
and why did the writer emphasize this?

Comparison of Ministries (Hebrews 8:3-6)
3 For every high priest is appointed to offer both gifts and sacrifices. Therefore it is necessary that this One also have something to offer. 4 For if He were on earth, He would not be a priest, since there are priests who offer the gifts according to the law; 5 who serve the copy and shadow of the heavenly things, as Moses was divinely instructed when he was about to make the tabernacle. For He said, "See that you make all things according to the pattern shown you on the mountain." 6 But now He has obtained a more excellent ministry, inasmuch as He is also Mediator of a better covenant, which was established on better promises.

We noted in Hebrews 5:1 that human high priests offered gifts and sacrifices. The writer now wanted his readers to pause and consider, "What does Jesus offer?"

As this letter was written, earthly priests still served in the sanctuary of the Jerusalem temple. This, like the tabernacle Moses built, was only a "copy and shadow of the heavenly things." [114] Sisters, put on your Old Testament glasses. The writer is going to review temporary elements of the Jewish system and then compare these earthly copies with the heavenly realities.

Levitical priests performed their service in a special two-room area. It was called the "sanctuary," translated from the Greek phrase "the holy place." Only priests were allowed there. Dividing the two rooms was a large, heavy curtain. The innermost room was called the Most Holy Place (or Holy of Holies). Only the high priest could enter this room and only once a year (Hebrews 9:7). On the Day of Atonement, he entered—though not without a washing, special robes, and sacrificial blood—and then he stood before the presence of God (Exodus 25:8). The veil that guarded this room acted as a barrier between God and the people. When Jesus died, this veil was torn from top to bottom, representing open access to the Father through Christ.

The tabernacle and its sanctuary were copies of the heavenly originals. What are the heavenly, original "tabernacle" and "sanctuary"? The true tabernacle is the church, and the sanctuary is heaven. Scholars assert that the sanctuary, "the true 'holy of holies,' is where Christ serves in the presence of God." [115] Compare these facts: (1) earthly priests had to go through the tabernacle to enter the sanctuary, and (2) the only way for us to enter into heaven is through the church. [116] Scripture says that (1) the Lord, not man, erected the true tabernacle (Hebrews 8:2); (2) Christ built the church (Matthew 16:18); and (3) there is no tabernacle in heaven (Revelation 21:22). Another comparison is that only priests could go into the sanctuary, and when we are baptized into Christ, we become spiritual priests (1 Peter 2:5, 9). We are therefore eligible to enter God's presence—in prayer while we live on earth and in heaven when we die.

Compare the copies and the heavenly
originals of the sanctuary and tabernacle.

Both the copies and originals were designed by God. The copies were required to follow His pattern. Before Moses assembled the physical elements of the tabernacle, God said, "See that you make all things according to the pattern shown you on the mountain," and Moses obeyed (Hebrews 8:5; cf. Exodus 25:8-9, 40). God expected obedience in the type and shadow of heavenly things, and He expects us to follow His specific instructions for worship in the true tabernacle (the church).

Although it was grand, the earthly tabernacle was temporary. It served its purpose. After Jesus shed His blood sacrifice, there was no more need for earthly priests. Lightfoot concluded,

> Jesus as high priest in the new age performs His service in the real, heavenly sanctuary. ... A sanctuary is a real sanctuary only if God is there. And that is precisely what makes the heavenly sanctuary, where Christ ministers, the real one. From this it follows that Christ's priestly service, performed in the presence of God, outranks that of His predecessors.[117]

Hebrews 8:6 reveals, "But now He has obtained a more excellent ministry, inasmuch as He is also Mediator of a better covenant, which was established on better promises."

Mediator. Jesus' more excellent ministry includes acting on our behalf as a "mediator"—that is, a person who stands in the middle between two parties, serving as intercessor or reconciler. Moses was the mediator through whom God gave the first covenant (Old Law) to Israel (Galatians 3:19; Hebrews 9:19). But in these last days, God spoke through His Son to mediate a new covenant (1:2; 12:24). Paul proclaimed, "For there is one God and one Mediator between God and men, the Man Christ Jesus" (1 Timothy 2:5). Lightfoot commented on His role as Mediator: "He stands in the middle between God and man, the ideal representative for both parties; and by His presence He not only mediates the new covenant but pledges the fulfillment of it."[118]

Christ, as our Mediator, "stands in the middle between God and man, the ideal representative for both parties."

Better Promises. As Mediator, Jesus guarantees the fulfillment of God's promises on which the better covenant was established. In our Christian journey, these promises include mercy, comfort, access to God, intercession, and the forgiveness of sins. And in that better place, God still offers eternal, spiritual rest. This offer has always been open, even to those under the Law of Moses. But the Hebrews readers, and we today, have a better Mediator and a better covenant.

How have we, like the Hebrews readers, neglected study and lost sight of Jesus as the better Mediator and of God's better promises?

COMPARISON OF COVENANTS (HEBREWS 8:7-13)

Have you ever wondered why the two parts of the Bible are called the Old Testament and the New Testament? The Greek term translated "covenant" in Hebrews 8:6 is a form of *diatheke*, meaning "last will and testament."[119] It is translated "testament" in Hebrews 9:16-17. This concept helps us see why the first covenant (by Moses) was described in the Old Testament and the new covenant (by Christ) was explained in the New Testament. Lenski clarified,

> The law brought to Israel by Moses is also called a testament and as such is also sealed with blood (9:15-20), but only with the blood of calves and goats. This law-testament was temporal and came to an end. The law came in 430 years after the testament that was made for Abraham (Gal. 3:17); and Israel lost its promises because of transgression so that this law-testament came to an end. ... Death alone puts a testament into force. God cannot die, but Jesus, God's Son, can and did, and thus the testament of God stands legally in force.[120]

The old covenant (testament) began with God's promises to Abraham. These included a great land, a great nation, a great name, and a great blessing for all nations through his seed (Genesis 12:1-3). The first three were fulfilled through the old covenant with Israel. The fourth promise was fulfilled as a spiritual blessing through Jesus in the new covenant (Galatians 3:19, 29). So we do not live under the laws of the Old Testament, but under those of the New Testament.

God fulfilled the four promises He made in the Abrahamic covenant. What were they, and how does this encourage all who live under the new covenant?

After God's people agreed to the covenant at Mount Sinai, they began to drift, doubt, and become dull of hearing. They complained and wanted to go back to Egypt. When they rebelled at the edge of the Promised Land, they were not allowed to enter. The Hebrews writer warned readers not to imitate those flawed people living under an inadequate covenant.

Flawed People, Inadequate Covenant (Hebrews 8:7-9)
7 *For if that first covenant had been faultless, then no place would have been sought for a second.* **8** *Because finding fault with them, He says: "Behold, the days are coming, says the LORD, when I will make a new covenant with the house of Israel and with the house of Judah—***9** *not according to the covenant that I made with their fathers in the day when I took them by the hand to lead them out of the land of Egypt; because they did not continue in My covenant, and I disregarded them, says the LORD."*

Hebrews 8:7-9 reiterates the necessity for a new covenant, for the first was inadequate (7:11, 18; Galatians 3:19-21). The Law of Moses was a ritualistic, temporary fix for sin. Its mortal, imperfect priests offered animals that did not remove sin. But the new covenant—guaranteed by God's oath and promise with Jesus as Mediator and Surety—provides better promises. This message was repeated over and over in the letter so that the immature, dull of hearing readers would get it! Let us also read the letter carefully so that we will get it too.

The writer quoted the words from another Old Testament prophecy: Jeremiah 31:31-34. Perhaps you remember this one too. God allowed the prophet, Jeremiah, to experience Judah's fall and Babylonian exile and then to give comfort: "There is hope in your future" (v. 17). Hebrews 8:8 quotes this prophecy concerning the better covenant God would make with His people: "Behold, the days are coming, says the LORD, when I will make a new covenant with the house of Israel and with the house of Judah" (Jeremiah 31:31).

Why did the Lord name both Israel and Judah? They were united as one nation when He first made His covenant with them. But under the harsh rule of Solomon's son, Rehoboam, they split. Ten tribes went north, made Jeroboam their king, and kept the name "Israel." Two tribes (Judah and Benjamin) remained with King Rehoboam and took the name of the larger tribe, "Judah." Israel broke covenant with God and, in 722 B.C., was captured by Assyria. Eventually, Judah's disobedience ended God's patience, and He allowed the Babylonians to conquer the nation around 586 B.C.

Therefore, when Jeremiah referred to both Israel and Judah, he was prophesying that one day all of God's people would be united into one body, the church (Ephesians 1:22-23; 2:14-16). In this "spiritual Israel," all are one in Christ Jesus (Galatians 3:28). Milligan summarized God's plan: "In the last days, under the reign of the Messiah, God would himself complete and bestow upon the house of Israel and upon the house of Judah the arrangement (*diatheke*) which, though hid for ages, was really intended from the beginning for the benefit of mankind."[121] Sisters, it is wonderful that, just as God's people were united at one time in the nation of Israel, His people are now united in the church—and we are part of it!

How might this reminder of oneness in Christ have helped
Jewish readers? How should the concept help people today?

God differentiates the two covenants by describing the new one as *not* "the covenant that I made with their fathers in the day when I took them by the hand to lead them out of the land of Egypt" (Hebrews 8:9). Through Moses, God lovingly led them out of bondage, supplied their needs, and committed to a relationship as their God (Exodus 6:7). But they rebelled. Lightfoot summed up Old Testament history as the "perpetual failure of Israel to live up to the terms agreed upon in the covenant. God was willing. And He was fully able to keep His end of the bargain. ... But 'they did not continue in my covenant, so I paid no heed to them, says the Lord.'"[122] Readers knew what had happened to their ancestors. They needed to consider the spiritual consequences if they were to fall away too. We would do well to pay attention also.

What consequences might we face if we drift, doubt,
and become dull of hearing? What will happen if we fall
completely away from our journey to that better place?

Heart versus Stone (Hebrews 8:10)
10 *For this is the covenant that I will make with the house of Israel after those days, says the LORD: I will put My laws in their mind and write them on their hearts; and I will be their God, and they shall be My people.*

Jeremiah pointed out the inadequacies of the Law of Moses and Israel. The Law of Moses was based on externals. It lacked the power and depth to spiritually change lives.[123] The people of Israel drifted, doubted, and became dull of hearing toward God's Word. But, as Jeremiah predicted, the new covenant is better! The word "new" (*kainos*) implies "a brand new kind."[124] This new covenant, established in the New Testament, is not an external and ritualistic list of i's to be dotted and t's to be crossed. It contains life-giving power to change hearts. It motivates spiritual growth and commitment and assures complete forgiveness of sins. The Hebrew saints, as well as Christians today, share in this blessing. The reason for the heart-changing results is revealed in Hebrews 8:10.

God's new laws are in our hearts! At Mount Sinai, God inscribed old laws on tablets of stone. The first set was broken physically by Moses in anger over Israel's sin. This was when Aaron made the golden calf. A second inscription was later broken spiritually by unbelieving hearts (Hebrews 3:12). But God keeps His promises. From a Judean mount, Jesus' sermon introduced new laws to replace old, external regulations. He quoted the old laws and asserted, "But I say to you." He clarified them as principles that spring from spiritual hearts.

The Old Testament law served God's purposes. However, no one but Jesus could live up to its standards. The New Testament has standards too. But while God's people complied with the Old Law by simply not committing murder or adultery, Jesus said we must not even do these in our heart. Laws inscribed in hearts and minds, instead of stone, can change people from the inside out. When we learn and live by New Testament principles, we appreciate our blessings in Christ and are motivated to obey. We view Christianity as a "get to" more than a "have to" religion. Thompson appropriately offered, "A church can never survive on a barrage of demands alone. The demands mean nothing if we do not realize that we possess a gift worth preserving. Consequently, exhortation must always be accompanied with reminders of what the church has been given."[125]

---

*Contrast the stone-inscribed old laws with the power
of the new covenant. Why should we see ours as
a "get to" more than a "have to" religion?*

The Hebrews writer next presented some wonderful new covenant blessings. Christians can enjoy the loving relationship God wanted with Israel: "I will be their God, and they shall be My people" (Hebrews 8:10). We know the Lord and are guilt-free from our sins.

Covenant Gifts for Christians (Hebrews 8:11-12)
11 *None of them shall teach his neighbor, and none his brother, saying, "Know the LORD," for all shall know Me, from the least of them to the*

greatest of them. 12 For I will be merciful to their unrighteousness, and their sins and their lawless deeds I will remember no more.

Christians enjoy a special knowledge and relationship with God. Under the old covenant, people were born into Israel as children of God, and then they were taught about Him (Deuteronomy 6:6-7). But it is just the opposite in the New Testament: people must first learn about God, and then they can become His children. They are taught and then baptized into His church family (Matthew 28:19). The former covenant involved a fleshly birth; the latter, a birth of water and Spirit (John 3:5). God begets us by the word of truth (James 1:18). So we must first gain knowledge of Him, and then, as Christians, we all know Him through a special relationship, "from the least of them to the greatest."

New Testament saints show knowledge of God through obedience, love, and good works (1 John 4:8; Titus 1:16). There is no need for one Christian brother to teach another the basic knowledge about God and how to have a relationship with Him (1 John 2:27). Each has already learned it in order to obey the gospel. But we must continue to grow in knowledge through Bible study (2 Peter 3:18). In the old covenant, not all enjoyed this privilege. It was basically the priests and scribes who read the Scriptures and shared it. In the new, there is no man or veil to keep people from God and His Word. Sisters, we are blessed with unlimited access today! Lenski summarized,

> The complete revelation came in Jesus, God's Son. After Pentecost the Spirit spread it far and wide. Although it was at first transmitted in the old, imperfect way this complete revelation was soon fixed for all time in a final canon to which all have full and free access. We are no longer dependent on merely what one may hear from another. No new prophets appear with new messages. We have all of God's word; and each has it in his own hand. We can by it even test those who stand up to preach and teach it.[126]

Discuss the privilege of having full access to God's Word in our hands today. Why is it important to test it against the words of those who preach and teach it?

With such wonderful blessings, why would the readers have wanted to return to their old Jewish religion? Christians enjoy privileges that the Israelites never experienced. Their sins were never fully taken out of the way during their lifetime. Their continual offerings were guilt-infused "reminders of sin every year" (Hebrews 10:3). But Christ's once-for-all sacrifice removes all trespasses (7:27), and God promises, "I will be merciful to their unrighteousness, and their sins and their iniquities will I remember no more" (10:17 KJV). Christians have a special knowledge and relationship with God, along with full and everlasting forgiveness.

Obsolete Old Covenant (Hebrews 8:13)
13 *In that He says, "A new covenant," He has made the first obsolete. Now what is becoming obsolete and growing old is ready to vanish away.*

The Hebrews writer concluded that the very description "new covenant" implied replacement of the old. With heart-changing laws and sin-removing efficacy, the new covenant made the old one obsolete, meaning "no longer useful."

The Old Testament no longer offers a valid religious system, but we can learn from it (Romans 15:4). The Hebrews accounts from Israel's history and messianic prophecies encourage and warn readers to persevere in the faith. They show that Christ is a better High Priest and Mediator of a better covenant. We enjoy its blessings today.

What do Jesus' high priesthood, the original sanctuary, and the true tabernacle mean to you in your Christian journey?

SUMMARY AND LOOKING FORWARD TO THE NEXT CHAPTER

The main point of Hebrews 8 is that we have a uniquely qualified High Priest who serves as Minister of the sanctuary (heaven) and true tabernacle (the church). The ministry of earthly priests is no longer needed. Jesus has a more excellent ministry as Mediator of a new covenant, established on better promises. Jeremiah prophesied that God would unite all His people with this new covenant and write its life-changing laws on their hearts. Hebrews 9 contrasts even more strongly the sanctuary and sacrifices of the old and new covenants. This letter serves as a reminder that Christ, as our High Priest, is the only guide on our journey to that better place.

CHAPTER 9

ASK FOR DIRECTIONS
(HEBREWS 9)

One of the perils of traveling is getting lost. Has this happened to you? One of our sons became lost very late one night in Memphis, Tennessee. He called us at home to ask for directions. We laid out a map and guided him to the interstate. We were thankful he asked for help. Some people do not want to ask. They may be embarrassed or prideful. But it is okay to ask. In many cases, it is the only way to know if you are on the right road. Asking questions is also the way to be sure we are on the right path to heaven.

We should not be afraid to ask questions about God, Christ, Scripture, the plan of salvation, or living the Christian life. The Bible provides answers. What issues do you struggle with? For many years, I wondered but felt guilty for asking, "Why did Jesus have to die?" This could have been an issue for discouraged, first-century Jewish converts. Lenski wrote, "A dead Messiah was beginning to look like no Messiah to them."[127]

Sisters, have you ever wondered why Jesus had to die? Have you ever asked, "Couldn't God have made a different plan of salvation?" Jesus essentially asked His Father this question in Gethsemane when He said, "If it is possible, let this cup pass from Me" (Matthew 26:39). He received an answer: there was no other way. The inspired Hebrews writer explained that Jesus' death was necessary. Sin atonement has always required blood. It was shed when inaugurating the first covenant, and it was an essential element in the New Testament. What can wash away my sin? Nothing but the blood of Jesus. His body and the sacrifice of animals were compared in Hebrews 9, along with the two covenants. This will help us understand why Jesus had to die.

OLD COVENANT ELEMENTS (HEBREWS 9:1-10)

Distinct differences exist between the Jewish religion and Christianity. The Hebrews writer did not belittle his readers' old faith system. Instead, he noted, "Even the first covenant had ordinances of divine service and the earthly sanctuary" (Hebrews 9:1). It served its purpose—to prepare humanity for the Christian age. Those living under Judaism learned many good things: moral principles, respect for God, and a desire for salvation. But that system was not able to take away sin. Old Testament rituals were inferior to New Testament realities and took place in an earthly sanctuary. The term "earthly" pertains to this perishable world and reveals a difference from the original, heavenly holy place.[128] Rituals performed under the Law of Moses were merely shadows of true Christian worship in spirit and truth (John 4:23). But they were magnificent shadows.

> *Tabernacle Furniture (Hebrews 9:1-5)*
> **1** *Then indeed, even the first covenant had ordinances of divine service and the earthly sanctuary.* **2** *For a tabernacle was prepared: the first part, in which was the lampstand, the table, and the showbread, which is called the sanctuary;* **3** *and behind the second veil, the part of the tabernacle which is called the Holiest of All,* **4** *which had the golden censer and the ark of the covenant overlaid on all sides with gold, in which were the golden pot that had the manna, Aaron's rod that budded, and the tablets of the covenant;* **5** *and above it were the cherubim of glory overshadowing the mercy seat. Of these things we cannot now speak in detail.*

We can only imagine the grandeur of the tabernacle built by Moses. The God-given pattern of richly colored tapestries and elements overlaid in gold inspired pride in the Israelites. The Hebrews letter reminded readers of the furniture in this holy tent, specifically the two-part holy area called the sanctuary.

Find a diagram of the Jewish tabernacle to better visualize the writer's description of this earthly structure, and discuss its main elements.

The writer led a tour through the two rooms in which only priests could enter. In the first room, there was a seven-armed lampstand and a table with twelve cakes of unleavened bread. The innermost room, the Most Holy Place, was where the high priest entered God's presence on the Day of Atonement. This room was described as having the golden censer and the ark of the covenant.[129] This furniture had great significance.

Just as Jewish rituals were a type of future Christian worship, tabernacle furniture can be compared to elements in the church. The continually burning lamps may represent the Christian's influence and the light of the gospel (Exodus 27:20; Psalm 119:105; Matthew 5:14-16).The showbread, eaten by priests, may compare with the spiritual bread eaten by Christians, priests of God (Matthew 4:4; John 6:35; 1 Peter 2:5, 9) and the Lord's Supper (Matthew 26:26; Acts 20:7). Sweet-smelling incense from the golden censer can represent our prayers and songs of praise (Psalm 141:2; Hebrews 13:15; Revelation 5:8; 8:4). The ark of the covenant may symbolize God's throne, where Christians may boldly go in prayer (Hebrews 4:16).[130]

Hebrews 9:4 names items within and upon the ark of the covenant. Inside were three items: "the golden pot that had the manna, Aaron's rod that budded, and the tablets of the covenant" (cf. Exodus 16:32-34). On top of the ark sat two golden cherubim with outstretched wings over its "propitiatory cover," the area representing God's presence.[131] Readers were familiar with these elements from the fuller accounts in Exodus 37 and 38. So the writer ended his brief description and moved on to discuss the tabernacle's function.

Why did the writer review the tabernacle and its elements?

Tabernacle Rituals (Hebrews 9:6-10)

6 *Now when these things had been thus prepared, the priests always went into the first part of the tabernacle, performing the services.* **7** *But into the second part the high priest went alone once a year, not without blood, which he offered for himself and for the people's sins committed in ignorance;* **8** *the Holy Spirit indicating this, that the way into the Holiest of All was not yet made manifest while the first tabernacle was still standing.* **9** *It was symbolic for the present time in which both gifts and sacrifices are offered which cannot make him who performed the service perfect in regard to the conscience—***10** *concerned only with foods and drinks, various washings, and fleshly ordinances imposed until the time of reformation.*

Priests and the rituals they performed in the earthly tabernacle had a purpose. They were inadequate to take away sin, but they symbolized Christ's role as High Priest and the effectual sacrifice. The writer now described the old covenant rituals.

Twice each day, priests entered the first room, the Holy Place, to offer incense on the altar and to trim the oil lamps (Exodus 30:7-8). Once a week, on the Sabbath, they ate the loaves and replaced them with fresh bread (Leviticus 24:5-9; Luke 6:4). Blood sacrifices were not offered here. This was done in the courtyard of the tabernacle, along with other daily offerings. They were also offered once a year in the Most Holy Place.

On the annual Day of Atonement, the high priest went alone through the veil into the Most Holy Place. He entered at least three times: first, to offer the blood of a young bull for his own sins (Leviticus 16:11); second, to offer sweet incense before the Lord (vv. 12-13); and third, after he was justified, to offer blood from the bull and a goat for unintentional sins of the people (vv. 18-19). Sins of defiance were excluded (Numbers 15:30-31). Blood sacrifices allowed worshipers to stand justified before God. Although these sacrifices atoned for sins, they did not remove them; therefore, Jesus' work exceeds that of the Jewish high priest.[132] How blessed we are that, through baptism, we are washed in the blood of the Lamb and free from all sin!

*Compare the sacrifice rituals of earthly
priests with the offering Jesus made.*

The Most Holy Place was a mysterious area. No one but the high priest laid eyes upon its contents. So during the centuries that "the first tabernacle was still standing," the way into the Most Holy Place "was not yet made manifest" (Hebrews 9:8). This concept may also apply to the fact that, before the gospel, people did not understand its redemptive message. People only knew about the prophecies inspired by the Holy Spirit. When Jesus died on the cross, the veil of the temple was literally ripped apart. This symbolized the removal of barriers between God and men.

Until that heavy curtain was rent, the tabernacle (as well as the Jerusalem temple) remained a figure (object lesson) of God's plan for redemption. The gifts and sacrifices offered there symbolically pardoned sins but did not free the conscience of guilt. Only Christ's blood was able to do that. For those finding it difficult to forgive themselves, F.F. Bruce reassured, "The reader with a disturbed conscience is likely to find more help in Hebrews than in almost anywhere else in Scripture"[133] (cf. Hebrews 9:14; 10:22). In Christ, and only in Christ, we have forgiveness and salvation.

The tabernacle, priests, and Jewish rituals concerned the earthly, perishable world. Along with the gifts and sacrifices, there were rules regarding food, drink, and ceremonial washings. These included laws on clean and unclean foods and drink along with ritualistic cleansings for priests, healed lepers, those who touched a dead body, female uncleanness, certain clothing, wooden dishes, and more (Exodus 30:19-20; Leviticus 6:27-28; 10:9; 11; 14:8-9; 16:4, 24; Numbers 6:2-3; 8:6-7; 19:11-12; Deuteronomy 14). Lightfoot concluded, "So many washings and nothing made clean."[134] These were all temporary, external ordinances of the flesh to symbolize the internal, moral purity required in the "time of reformation" (Hebrews 9:10). This means the Christian age, which began in A.D. 33 and will last until Jesus' second coming.

Discuss the quote "So many washings and nothing made clean."

New Covenant Sanctuary and Sacrifice (Hebrews 9:11-15)
11 *But Christ came as High Priest of the good things to come, with the greater and more perfect tabernacle not made with hands, that is, not of this creation.* **12** *Not with the blood of goats and calves, but with His own blood He entered the Most Holy Place once for all, having obtained eternal redemption.* **13** *For if the blood of bulls and goats and the ashes of a heifer, sprinkling the unclean, sanctifies for the purifying of the flesh,* **14** *how much more shall the blood of Christ, who through the eternal Spirit offered Himself without spot to God, cleanse your conscience from dead works to serve the living God?* **15** *And for this reason He is the Mediator of the new covenant, by means of death, for the redemption of the transgressions under the first covenant, that those who are called may receive the promise of the eternal inheritance.*

Hebrew 9:11-15 is called "the heart of Hebrews."[135] In the Greek manuscript, verses 11 and 12 form one long sentence exalting Christ as our High Priest and better, once-for-all sacrifice. Slowly, reread this beautiful passage, and visualize it as a summary of the entire Hebrews sermon.

First-century converts would have done well to tape this quote to their bathroom mirrors, kitchen windows, and chariot windshields as a reminder that Jesus is better! In fact, we need it too. These five verses explain why Jesus is our great High Priest and perfect sacrifice. When we obey Him in baptism, His blood washes away our sin and cleanses our conscience (1 Peter 3:21). When we continue to walk in the light (1 John 1:7), we are among the "called," who will receive the promise of the eternal inheritance (Hebrews 9:15).

What does it mean to be "called"?
Read 2 Thessalonians 2:14 and 1 Peter 2:9.

The section of Hebrews in which chapter 9 falls is a comparison of the new and better covenant with the old, inadequate Jewish system. Here, the writer explained that Christ "came as High Priest of the good things to come, with the greater and more perfect tabernacle not made with hands" (Hebrews 9:11). The good things to come include all the spiritual blessings available in the Lord's church. The church is the "greater and more perfect tabernacle" for which the old was but a type and shadow. The Jewish system of worship (the first tabernacle) was replaced so that all people could become Christians (priests) and come boldly into God's presence. Milligan asserted, "The Old Tabernacle, with all that pertained to it fell to the ground; and on its ruins was erected the true Tabernacle of which Christ has become the prime Minister (8:2; 9:11)."[136] To encourage these Jewish Christians, the writer kept emphasizing the fact that Jesus and Christianity are better!

Human high priests entered an earthly sanctuary after offering the blood of calves for themselves and the blood of goats for the people. This ritual had to be done annually. But Christ shed His own blood once for all and then entered the true (original) sanctuary, the Most Holy Place called heaven. His sacrifice was better because it removed sin. The blood of bulls and goats was a type and shadow of the purifying blood of Jesus (Hebrews 9:13).

Readers understood the concept of purification. They knew about the Old Testament cleansing rituals of sprinkling both the blood of animals and ashes. Numbers 19 presents instructions to sprinkle the ashes of a heifer for impurities like touching a grave, a dead body, or an unclean person. These rituals cleansed the physical body, but did nothing for the guilty conscience. Consider which is worse: to be physically defiled or spiritually unclean? Readers were asked to bear in mind that if the ritual sprinkling of blood and ashes was enough to satisfy requirements of physical purification, "how much more shall the blood of Christ" cleanse their conscience from sin to serve the living God (Hebrews 9:14)? Much, much more! His was a better sacrifice.

Compare the Jewish ritual of physical washing
with Christian baptism. Read 1 Peter 3:21.

His was a perfect sacrifice. Hebrews 9:14 describes Christ as one "who through the eternal Spirit offered Himself without spot to God." Although "Spirit" is capitalized in some translations, scholars assert that this was not a reference to the Holy Spirit. It was Jesus' own internal spirit that volunteered as sacrifice. John 10:17-18 reveals that no man was able to take His life. He gave it. Only the blood of a perfect, unblemished victim would do (Leviticus 1:3, 10). Jesus fit that requirement, for He was "spotless in the inward and moral sense, an indispensable requirement for a spiritual sacrifice."[137] Not one sin had stained His life.

Therefore, as Hebrews 9:15 explains, Christ's sacrificial death qualified Him to become Mediator of the new covenant, covering the sins of all who are called (cf. 2 Thessalonians 2:14). Because of Christ's sacrifice, all the faithful are able to "receive the promise of the eternal inheritance." Sisters, because of our obedience to the gospel, we are among those "called"! And we will receive His promised eternal inheritance if we persevere.

Jesus: Mediator of the New Covenant (Hebrews 9:16-17)
16 *For where there is a testament, there must also of necessity be the death of the testator.* **17** *For a testament is in force after men are dead, since it has no power at all while the testator lives.*

The preceding verses set the stage to answer the question "Why did Jesus have to die?" Hebrews 9:16-22 presents two reasons: (1) for the forgiveness of sins (v. 15) and (2) because a will becomes in force only after its maker dies (v. 16). First, only the blood of a perfect sacrificial Lamb could have redeemed us from transgressions. Sin came at a price. The blood of bulls and goats was not able to pay it. Jesus' blood could and did, so "God can now be just in justifying every true believer."[138] Second, the old covenant (testament) was inadequate and had to be replaced by the new. Only after a death can a will and testament become a reality and an inheritance be claimed. Jesus' death allowed His new will and testament to go into effect and paid the price of sin, making available our inheritance of eternal life.

Jesus gave Himself to die in order to establish His new covenant (testament). This new covenant is better, for it took away even the sins of faithful men and women who lived under the old. Sisters, have you ever wondered how those good people were justified? We learn in James 2:21-25 that Abraham and Rahab were justified by their obedience to God. One commentary noted, "The cross provides salvation for all the obedient believers of all times."[139] Jesus' sacrifice had power and efficacy that animal sacrifices did not. It was retroactive, reaching back to the beginning of time and fulfilling the promise made to Abraham that through his seed all nations of the earth would be blessed—past, present, and future. Abraham received this promise, as do Christians today (Matthew 8:10-11). Pace summarized,

> Divine conditions had to be met in order for God to offer salvation to His people. All of these were fulfilled by Christ's blood. His death put into effect the new covenant. His blood took away sins—not only the sins of Christians, but also the sins of the faithful ones of the Old Testament who offered the animal sacrifices year after year, anticipating God's perfect sacrifice. By allowing His blood to cleanse the "copies" of heavenly things, Christ has enabled us to enter into the true presence of God.[140]

Hebrews 9:16-17 clearly explains why Jesus had to die. The New Testament (covenant) could not have been established until He, as the testator, shed His blood in death. As the writer was about to explain more fully, blood was an essential element of all God's covenants.

Explain why the new covenant is called Jesus'
will and testament. What is our inheritance?

Inauguration with Blood (Hebrews 9:18-22)
18 *Therefore not even the first covenant was dedicated without blood.* **19** *For when Moses had spoken every precept to all the people according to the law, he took the blood of calves and goats, with water, scarlet wool, and hyssop, and sprinkled both the book itself and all the people,* **20** *saying, "This is the blood of the covenant which God has commanded you."* **21** *Then likewise he sprinkled with blood both the tabernacle and all the*

vessels of the ministry. **22** *And according to the law almost all things are purified with blood, and without shedding of blood there is no remission.*

When the first covenant was established with Israel, blood was included. Hebrews 9:18-22 summarizes the Exodus 24:1-8 and 40:9-15 accounts. Exodus 24:1-8 explains that, at the ratification of the first covenant, Moses sprinkled blood on the altar, the book, and the people. In the account of the tabernacle dedication, oil was mentioned, but not blood (40:9-15). Hebrews 9:21 reveals that blood *was* involved. More evidence is provided by the Jewish historian Josephus. In *Antiquities* 3.8.6, he wrote that the tabernacle and vessels were consecrated with "fragrant oil" and "with the blood of bulls and goats." Aaron and his sons were sanctified as priests with the blood of a ram (Leviticus 8:30).

It is interesting to compare the phrase "This is the blood of the covenant" (Hebrews 9:20; Exodus 24:8) with Jesus' words in 1 Corinthians 11:25. In the upper room with His disciples, He established an element of the Lord's Supper that represented His blood. It was the fruit of the vine. He "took the cup after supper, saying, 'This cup is the new covenant in My blood. This do, as often as you drink it, in remembrance of Me'" (cf. Matthew 26:27-28). We are to do this on the first day of the week until He comes again (Acts 20:7). When I was a child, I heard a sermon that prompted me to always look in three directions while partaking: backward to the day of Christ's crucifixion and death, inward with repentance and thankfulness for forgiveness of sins, and forward to the day when Christ comes again.

What do you think about when taking the Lord's Supper?

Notice the writer's observation that "almost all things are purified with blood" (Hebrews 9:22). In many of the cleansing processes, water and fire were used (Numbers 19:6-7). But for ceremonies involving forgiveness of sins, blood was always involved. Leviticus 17:11 states, "It is the blood that makes atonement for the soul." Hebrews 9:22 adds, "without shedding of blood there is no remission." The Old Testament sacrifices served a purpose only because God connected the animal blood with the bloody death of Christ.[141] In order for people to have sins forgiven and to inherit eternal life, Jesus had to die.

Once-for-All Sacrifice (Hebrews 9:23-26)
23 *Therefore it was necessary that the copies of the things in the heavens should be purified with these, but the heavenly things themselves with better sacrifices than these.* **24** *For Christ has not entered the holy places made with hands, which are copies of the true, but into heaven itself, now to appear in the presence of God for us;* **25** *not that He should offer Himself often, as the high priest enters the Most Holy Place every year with blood of another—***26** *He then would have had to suffer often since the foundation of the world; but now, once at the end of the ages, He has appeared to put away sin by the sacrifice of Himself.*

The last few verses of Hebrews 9 summarize the superiority of Jesus' sacrifice over those in the old Jewish system. The writer pointed out that animal sacrifices (along with water and ashes) secured a temporary, symbolical cleansing of the tent, its elements, and human flesh. But as Milligan asserted, "It served only to demonstrate the extremely polluting nature of sin, and the great necessity of that real spiritual cleansing which can be effected only through the infinitely precious blood of Christ (1 John 1:7)."[142] The blood of bulls and goats cleansed copies of heavenly things, but Jesus' blood cleansed the true elements of the spiritual kingdom—the souls of penitent believers. Inward cleansing is necessary to become a child of God, to be a fit habitation for God,[143] and after death, to enter the true sanctuary called heaven.

In contrast to the Levitical priests, Christ did not have to go into the earthly sanctuary made with hands in order to perform priestly duties. He entered the sanctuary of heaven with His own blood, and in the presence of God, He procured our pardon. Sisters, how blessed we are! How grateful we should be!

Contrast the symbolical cleansing under the old covenant with the inward cleansing we enjoy.

Earthly priests poured out the inadequate blood of bulls and goats, but the blood of Jesus justifies all who believe and obey. Earthly high priests had to annually perform the sacrificial rites, but Jesus offered Himself once and for all. His offering ushered in the Christian age.

One Death, Then Judgment (Hebrews 9:27-28)
27 *And as it is appointed for men to die once, but after this the judgment,* **28** *so Christ was offered once to bear the sins of many. To those who eagerly wait for Him He will appear a second time, apart from sin, for salvation.*

Now we understand that Jesus had to die. But He had to die only once. Death is an appointment everyone must keep.

The Greek word for "appointed" in Hebrews 9:27 means "reserved or certain for someone, one is destined."

Has God set an expiration date for each of us? No. The Greek word for "appointed" here means "reserved or certain for someone, one is destined" (Colossians 1:5; 2 Timothy 4:8a).[144]

Each of us will taste death, unless we are alive when Christ comes again (1 Thessalonians 4:16-17). Pace offered, "Man is born once, lives once, dies once, and then faces judgment once, just as Christ was once offered and will appear once more."[145] Judgment is an appointment we all will keep.

What will that day be like? It will be a sad day for those whose sins are not forgiven and for wayward children of God who drift, doubt, become dull of hearing, and quit their Christian journey. But it will be glorious for the faithful who persevere to the end. We eagerly anticipate His second coming to receive our eternal rest and reward. Pace wrote, "When guilt is removed and one understands that he is forgiven, he can eventually lose the fear of facing God through death. What do the innocent have to fear? One can be calm and peaceful in all calamities when he is aware by faith that he has no guilt before God."[146] This gives us assurance that we are saved, we are on the right path, and we have the answer to our question, "Why did Jesus have to die?"

How does Hebrews 9:27-28 affect your feelings about death?

SUMMARY AND LOOKING FORWARD TO THE NEXT CHAPTER

Some on the Christian journey wonder, "Why did Jesus have to die?" The Hebrews writer explained that blood was an essential element in atonement for sin. But animal blood, the sanctuary, and sacrifices under the Law of Moses were merely shadows of true Christian redemption. They symbolically pardoned sins, but did not free the conscience of guilt. The blood of Jesus did. His death allowed His new will and testament to come into effect. Therefore, those who are faithful and obedient, from all times and all nations, can inherit God's promise of eternal life. Jesus' death was necessary.

What will we learn in Hebrews 10? In verses 1-18, the author completed the central part of this letter, which concerned the superiority of Christ's priesthood. Then, he began the practical section of this letter by explaining our responsibilities and privileges as New Testament Christians.

CHAPTER 10

WALK WITH ONE ANOTHER
(HEBREWS 10)

There is safety in numbers, especially when we travel. On long trips, a companion can watch your back and help if you get lost or tired. When my sisters and I were young, our mother attempted to drive from North Carolina to visit her parents in Texas. When we stopped in Atlanta, she was unable to complete the trip. We were too young to help then, but recently, my sister, Judi, and I took turns driving our parents that same route to visit Grandmother. This trip was full of laughter and fellowship, and we felt safe.

Scripture refers to the benefits of traveling together. Solomon wrote, "Two are better than one ... for if they fall, one will lift up his companion" (Ecclesiastes 4:9-10). This is true in our Christian walk. In the middle of Hebrews 10, the writer began a practical section urging us to walk together with love, good deeds, and fellowship. But, first, he wrapped up his theological discussion of Christ's superior sacrifice.

SACRIFICES COMPARED (HEBREWS 10:1-10)

When Adam and Eve disobeyed God, He required animal sacrifices to cover sin. Each family became responsible for offerings until the Old Law was established through Moses. Under that law, Levitical priests made daily, weekly, monthly, and yearly offerings. But these rituals and that blood could not take away sin.

Insufficiency of Levitical Offerings (Hebrews 10:1-4)
1 *For the law, having a shadow of the good things to come, and not the very image of the things, can never with these same sacrifices, which they offer continually year by year, make those who approach perfect.* **2** *For then would they not have ceased to be offered? For the worshipers, once purified, would have had no more consciousness of sins.* **3** *But in those sacrifices there is a reminder of sins every year.* **4** *For it is not possible that the blood of bulls and goats could take away sins.*

When you were a child, did you ever try to catch your shadow? It cannot be done. People are real, but shadows are not. The dark outline only represents reality. Hebrews uses this analogy to contrast the Law of Moses with the spiritual blessings in Christ. The writer informed his readers that their old Jewish religion and its tabernacle, sanctuary, priests, and sacrifices were merely shadows (temporary symbols) of the true religion, heaven, the church, and Christ Jesus.

Hebrews 10:1-4 reveals the inadequacy of these shadows in the Levitical system. They neither removed sin nor relieved the guilty conscience. If animal blood had been able to redeem, there would have been no need for sacrifices "continually year by year." One of the purposes of this frequent ritual was to remind people they were still sinners. However, those washed in Christ have no guilt. God remembers their sins no more (Hebrews 8:12). The book of Hebrews offers assurance that, when we are baptized, the blood of Christ cleanses us of sin. We are in a saved condition. Sisters, this gives us great comfort in a world so full of religious confusion!

Sufficiency of Christ's Sacrifice (Hebrews 10:5-10)
5 *Therefore, when He came into the world, He said: "Sacrifice and offering You did not desire, but a body You have prepared for Me.* **6** *In burnt offerings and sacrifices for sin You had no pleasure.* **7** *Then I said, 'Behold, I have come—in the volume of the book it is written of Me—to do Your will, O God.'"* **8** *Previously saying, "Sacrifice and offering, burnt offerings, and offerings for sin You did not desire, nor had pleasure in them" (which are offered according to the law),* **9** *then He said, "Behold, I have come to do Your will, O God." He takes away the first that He may establish the second.* **10** *By that will we have been sanctified through the offering of the body of Jesus Christ once for all.*

Animal sacrifices were only shadows of the forgiveness available through Christ's blood. It was God's plan before the foundation of the earth to send His Son at just the right time (Galatians 4:4). It has been suggested that, when God disclosed the need for a perfect human sacrifice for sin, the Son figuratively raised His hand and volunteered. The scenario can be seen in Hebrews 10:5-10. David's words (from Psalm 40:6-8) reveal "a kind of conversation between the eternal Son and God the Father."[147]

Here, David praised God for deliverance and offered to do His will. He also revealed the words of Christ. Notice the repetition of verses 5-7 and 8-9 in Hebrews 10. This is called Hebrew parallelism. In each section, the writer first named what God did not desire (sacrifices and offerings). These did not justify our sins. Then he told what was required to please God: "the offering of the body of Jesus Christ once for all" (v. 10). Sin is a terrible infection. It can keep us out of heaven and send us to hell. Only an exceptional sacrifice was able to cure.

Why is it significant that Christ voluntarily
offered Himself as our sacrifice for sin?

Final Contrasts (Hebrews 10:11-18)
11 *And every priest stands ministering daily and offering repeatedly the same sacrifices, which can never take away sins.* **12** *But this Man, after He had offered one sacrifice for sins forever, sat down at the right hand of God,* **13** *from that time waiting till His enemies are made His footstool.* **14** *For by one offering He has perfected forever those who are being sanctified.* **15** *But the Holy Spirit also witnesses to us; for after He had said before,* **16** *"This is the covenant that I will make with them after those days, says the* Lord: *I will put My laws into their hearts, and in their minds I will write them,"* **17** *then He adds, "Their sins and their lawless deeds I will remember no more."* **18** *Now where there is remission of these, there is no longer an offering for sin.*

How could readers not have realized the inadequacy of animal blood? How could they have forgotten that Jesus' once-for-all sacrifice provided true redemption? This section of verses is considered by some to be the climax of the entire Hebrews letter. As you read it, notice the contrasts between the old and new covenants.

Here, readers were reminded that Jewish priests worked continuously, but their tasks removed no sin. One writer asserted that the same sacrifices in the same place in the same way were "ever, ever at work; never, never doing any real good."[148] They merely symbolized Christ's better, one-time sacrifice.

The paragraph points out several contrasts: (1) Jewish priests continually offered sacrifices, while Jesus gave Himself once for all. (2) The priests stood to perform their duties and were still doing so at the time this letter was written. But when Christ Jesus finished His offering, He sat down at the right hand of God. (3) The animal blood poured out by Jewish priests was never able to take away sins, but Jesus' blood "has perfected forever those who are being sanctified" (Hebrews 10:14). Christ's was the last and better sacrifice. No more were necessary. He accomplished the will of God to provide a means of salvation. As a reward, He sits in an honored position at God's right hand, awaiting the day of judgment when all His enemies will be made His footstool (Hebrews 1:13; Psalm 110:1; 1 Corinthians 15:24-26).

It was always God's plan to replace the inadequate old covenant. Hebrews 10:15-16 reminded readers of the prophecy in Jeremiah 31:33-34. God had promised that in the new covenant He would put His laws into the hearts and minds of His people. There would be a life-changing component in the Christian age. Christ's blood would provide absolute forgiveness. Therefore, His people would no longer carry guilt. Their consciences would be clean. In Hebrews 10:17, God said, "Their sins and their lawless deeds I will remember no more." The section concludes, "Now where there is remission of these, there is no longer an offering for sin" (v. 18).

With this central portion and climax of the letter ended, readers were able to rest from their anxiety and their temptation to return to Judaism. It should have been clear to them that salvation was found only in Christ. So the writer began a new appeal for perseverance in the Christian journey, the only journey that leads to that better place.

Why did the writer spend so much time and
detail contrasting Judaism and Christianity?

Encouragement to Persevere (Hebrews 10:19-25)
19 *Therefore, brethren, having boldness to enter the Holiest by the blood of Jesus,* **20** *by a new and living way which He consecrated for us, through the veil, that is, His flesh,* **21** *and having a High Priest over the house of God,* **22** *let us draw near with a true heart in full assurance of faith, having our hearts sprinkled from an evil conscience and our bodies washed with pure water.* **23** *Let us hold fast the confession of our hope without wavering, for He who promised is faithful.* **24** *And let us consider one another in order to stir up love and good works,* **25** *not forsaking the assembling of ourselves together, as is the manner of some, but exhorting one another, and so much the more as you see the Day approaching.*

When we compare the first part of the Hebrews letter with what remains, we see a pattern that Paul followed in many of his letters. The first part contains a doctrinal section, and the second part offers practical application. The Hebrews writer had presented a powerful theological treatise on Christ's sacrifice. Now, he explained how to use this information. It is good to know biblical facts, but it is most valuable if we apply them to life.

Perhaps Fanny J. Crosby was meditating on Hebrews 10 when she wrote the words to "Blessed Assurance." We can sing with her about our spiritual condition as an "heir of salvation, purchase of God, born of His Spirit, washed in His blood." We have confidence that Christ's blood remits sins. Faithful first-century Christians were justified, cleansed in soul and conscience. We, as children of God today, can boldly say we have that same blessed assurance.

Jesus, our High Priest, rent the symbolic veil and removed the barrier between us and our Father. The writer began his practical section by reminding readers of this concept.

Is it not wonderful, sisters, that under the new covenant, as God's children, we can enter His presence through prayer? We have full assurance of acceptance and answer to our petitions (Hebrews 4:16; 10:19; 1 John 5:14-15). Surely the Jewish brethren, who had experienced restrictions in the physical temple, appreciated the privilege of entering the heavenly reality of the Most Holy Place. Christ's crucifixion opened the way, and as our High Priest, He made this entrance a new and living way to God (John 14:6).

This path is only available to members of God's household, the church. We have met two purifying conditions: (1) internally, our hearts were sprinkled to cleanse the guilty conscience, and (2) externally, our bodies were washed with water (Hebrews 10:22; 1 Peter 3:21; 1 John 1:7). These realities of repentance and baptism were represented in Jewish rituals. Priests sprinkled blood as a symbol for cleansing. They ceremoniously washed themselves with water before approaching God (Exodus 29:4; Leviticus 16:4). Under the new covenant, we must be cleansed by repentance and baptism before we can approach God.

Have you been washed in Christ's blood through baptism? Explain how this should affect your conscience and your prayer life.

The message that Christianity was better was just what weak and discouraged readers needed. The writer invited his readers to "draw near" to God with "full assurance of faith" (Hebrews 10:22; cf. James 1:6) and hold without wavering to the hope they professed. The original term for "without wavering" meant "not to let droop," like a banner flying high as a flag-bearer in battle makes sure the colors are seen.[149]

The original term for "without wavering" in Hebrews 10:23 meant "not to let droop," like a banner flying high in battle.

Whatever trials we face, we must boldly stand in faith. We have hope in God's promise of an eternal rest in heaven. This will help us persevere to the end.

God has provided special people in our journey to encourage us: our Christian brothers and sisters. We are "stirred up" by their love and support in worship and in fellowship (Hebrews 10:24-25). The term "stir up" (*paroxusmos*) means "provoking," "to encourage someone in love."[150] This verbal encouragement implies one person joining another on a journey and encouraging the traveler to keep pressing on despite obstacles and fatigue. We need one another.

When we neglect congregational gatherings, we miss the support they offer. Lightfoot proposed, "There is a vital connection between the expressions meet together and encouraging one another. The thought is not so much that they were to encourage one another to meet together, but that they were to meet together where such encouragement was available in the assembly."[151] Assembling is required by God not only for worship, but also for building one another up spiritually and emotionally. Paul stated that whenever Christians come together, they should "let all things be done for edification" (1 Corinthians 14:26).

What are some ways we can "stir up" our brothers and
sisters to encourage them on the Christian journey?

This support helps us in life's trials. It inspires faith and hope even more as we "see the Day approaching" (Hebrews 10:25). This refers to the day of judgment (1 Thessalonians 5:4; 2 Thessalonians 1:10). Having someone walk with us makes the journey easier, as does knowing that the end is not far away. The fact that Christ is coming soon should give us strength.

Warning against Despising the Word (Hebrews 10:26-31)
26 *For if we sin willfully after we have received the knowledge of the truth, there no longer remains a sacrifice for sins,* **27** *but a certain fearful expectation of judgment, and fiery indignation which will devour the adversaries.* **28** *Anyone who has rejected Moses' law dies without mercy on the testimony of two or three witnesses.* **29** *Of how much worse punishment, do you suppose, will he be thought worthy who has trampled the Son of God underfoot, counted the blood of the covenant by which he was sanctified a common thing, and insulted the Spirit of grace?* **30** *For we know Him who said, "Vengeance is Mine, I will repay," says the Lord. And again, "The*

LORD will judge His people." **31** *It is a fearful thing to fall into the hands of the living God.*

The Hebrews letter likely was based on a sermon, and in it, Jewish converts were admonished to beware of falling away into apostasy. At this point, the writer presented the fourth of five warnings:

- Do not *drift* from the Word—Hebrews 2:1-4 (neglect)
- Do not *doubt* the Word—Hebrews 3:7–4:13 (hard heart)
- Do not become *dull* toward the Word—Hebrews 5:11–6:20 (sluggishness)
- > Do not *despise* the Word—Hebrews 10:26-39 (willfulness)
- Do not *defy* the Word—Hebrews 12:25-29 (refusing to hear)

In Hebrews 2, he warned readers not to drift from God's Word. In Hebrews 3 and 4, he urged them not to imitate their Jewish ancestors, who had doubted God's promises. In Hebrews 5 and 6, he noted that their lack of Bible study had made them "dull of hearing," and he reminded them to follow Abraham's faith and assurance of hope. The Hebrew Christians had not fallen away completely. Drifting, doubting, and becoming dull of hearing are preliminary steps toward apostasy. These can happen to people with good hearts. People may not even realize they are beginning the downward spiral.

These actions can occur because of human weakness. We get busy, distracted, and weighed down by burdens that pull us away from God and His Word. But there is hope. Our priorities can be reset. We can be revitalized. Encouragement from fellow Christians and from our Mediator and High Priest can help pull us back into the right path (Hebrews 2:18; 4:16; 5:2).

Name some clues that a brother or sister is drifting,
doubting, dull of hearing, or despising the Word.
What can you do to encourage that person?

The next attitude (despising the Word) combined with deliberate and habitual sin is full-blown apostasy. And it is much harder to change. The writer gave a stern warning in Hebrews 10:26-31.

God has offered salvation. Jesus voluntarily gave His all for our heavenly rest. But if a Christian begins this journey and then purposely *continues* to sin, "there no longer remains a sacrifice for sins, but a certain fearful expectation of judgment, and fiery indignation which will devour the adversaries" (Hebrews 10:26-27). Milligan noted, "He not only shuts out himself from grace, but the door of repentance is shut behind him; and he has before him only the prospect of a damnation from which there is no escape."[152]

Consequences of presumptuous sin had been discussed. The writer referred to Old Testament atonement for ignorant and wayward sins, even for sins of passion. But no forgiveness was extended for rebellious sinning with "a high hand" (Leviticus 5:14-16; Numbers 15:28-31).[153] Under the Law of Moses, two or three witnesses condemned a person to death (Deuteronomy 17:6). No mercy or appeal was available. The writer asked, "Of how much worse punishment, do you suppose, will he be thought worthy" when he has blatantly rebelled against God's better plan and rejected Jesus' better sacrifice (Hebrews 10:29)? Lightfoot asked, "What greater crime can be imagined than to despise God's Son, regard His sacrifice as no more than an ordinary death, do outrage to His gracious Spirit, and all of this by one who once acknowledged Jesus as Lord?"[154]

Compare the punishment for deliberate
sin in the old and new covenants.

We pity those with such hardheartedness toward the Father, the Savior, and the Spirit. We want to help. We can set an example, encourage them, and pray for circumstances to change their hearts. But as we learned in Hebrews 6:4-6, "It is impossible ... to renew them again to repentance." They must want to change.

Sadly, the state in which they die is the state in which they will be judged. And God will render justice. Hebrews quotes Deuteronomy 32:35-36 in which God said, "Vengeance is Mine, and recompense ... the LORD will judge His people." Justice is part of God's character. He will reward and punish (Psalm 135:14; Romans 12:19). What a blessing for the faithful to anticipate entrance into His joy! But the unrepentant has only "a certain fearful expectation of judgment, and fiery indignation which will devour the adversaries" (Hebrews 10:27; cf. 2 Thessalonians 1:8-10). The writer exclaimed, "It is a fearful thing to fall into the hands of the living God" (Hebrews 10:31).

Sisters, do you remember fire-and-brimstone sermons? Preaching has, in general, become a kinder, gentler message. This has likely contributed to the shrinking number of believers and the rising number of atheists. Preachers have a responsibility to warn people about the consequences of rebellion and rejection. Lenski asserted, "By not frightening men into heaven they fail to frighten them away from hell."[155] This applies not only to men in the pulpit but also to members in the pew. Are we doing others good by never mentioning hell?

Explain the value of fire-and-brimstone sermons.

Strength in Persecution (Hebrews 10:32-34)
32 *But recall the former days in which, after you were illuminated, you endured a great struggle with sufferings: **33** partly while you were made a spectacle both by reproaches and tribulations, and partly while you became companions of those who were so treated; **34** for you had compassion on me in my chains, and joyfully accepted the plundering of your goods, knowing that you have a better and an enduring possession for yourselves in heaven.*

How did you feel when you were baptized? Likely you were filled with joy and a desire to tell everyone about Christ! It did not matter what anyone thought or said. You were on fire for the Lord. Perhaps you signed up for various activities in the Lord's work. It seemed so little compared to what He had done for us. If your enthusiasm has waned, what happened?

These Hebrews began their Christian journey with fervor. They were willing to stand up for Jesus, no matter the cost. But Satan had discouraged them. The writer asked them to think back to their conversion in Hebrews 10:32-34.

There is no mention of martyrdom or imprisonment among these readers. But the writer noted harassment and loss of property. At that time, it was a crime to show sympathy for persecuted Christians, and they had actively cared for the needs of their brothers and sisters.[156] This included ministering to those who were imprisoned (Hebrews 13:3). For their compassion, readers were "made a spectacle" (10:33). This meant they were exposed to public shame and insult (1 Corinthians 4:9).

Do you think this could happen to us? Already Christians are being jailed for their beliefs. Those who stand up for what is right are mocked in the media. Are we standing up for them and showing compassion? Will we also stand up under the threat of jail? Sisters, these are possibilities we need to consider.

Discuss some instances of Christians being "made a spectacle" today.

The early mindset of these readers was that they had "a better and an enduring possession" (Hebrews 10:34). But Satan's attacks had worn them down. Their lack of study and fellowship had discouraged them almost to the point of giving up. This letter was written to revive and remind them of their previous fervor. They needed encouragement to persevere.

What concepts in this letter strengthen you for enduring persecution?

Keep On Keeping On (Hebrews 10:35-39)

35 *Therefore do not cast away your confidence, which has great reward.* **36** *For you have need of endurance, so that after you have done the will of God, you may receive the promise:* **37** *"For yet a little while, and He who is coming will come and will not tarry.* **38** *Now the just shall live by faith; but if anyone draws back, my soul has no pleasure in him."* **39** *But we are not of those who draw back to perdition, but of those who believe to the saving of the soul.*

The writer praised his readers' previous bold stand. He now encouraged them to continue in their Christian journey. The phrase "cast away your confidence" was an allusion to weak soldiers who, in battle, would throw away their shields and flee from the enemy.[157] The writer urged readers to be strong in the Lord and stand in His promise (Hebrews 6:15). Perhaps their circumstances were similar to those of Habakkuk. He questioned God concerning how long the unrighteous would trample God's people. God's answer was "The just shall live by his faith" (Habakkuk 2:4). These words should inspire strength and perseverance.

The wait will not be long. Hebrews 10:37-38 offers hope in Christ's soon return. Two phrases—"yet a little while" and "will not tarry"—come from Isaiah 26:20 and Habakkuk 2:3-4. Jesus is coming soon. If we throw down our armor and retreat, God will not be pleased. He said to "faint not" (Galatians 6:9 KJV). Quitters will not receive the heavenly reward. Faithful Christians persevere. Therefore, we must be courageous. We must be faithful. We must stand our ground. And for this, we will enter the eternal rest. We want to hear Christ say, "Come, you blessed of My Father, inherit the kingdom prepared for you from the foundation of the world" (Matthew 25:34).

Jesus is coming soon. What impact should this have on your life?

SUMMARY AND LOOKING FORWARD TO THE NEXT CHAPTER

Hebrews 10 concludes the central part of this letter—that is, the discussion about Christ's superior sacrifice. The old covenant, its priests, and its sacrifices were inadequate. Jeremiah prophesied that it was God's plan to put new, better, and life-changing laws into the hearts of His people. Christ's once-for-all sacrifice justifies all who obey and allows us to draw near to God in full assurance of faith. Christians are warned not to despise God's Word and rebelliously sin, for there is no sacrifice left—only judgment and fire. Readers are encouraged to continue their good works and persevere. Do not quit! In the next chapter, famously called "Faith's Hall of Fame," we will see a list of Old Testament heroes and heroines who are worthy of imitation.

CHAPTER 11

VISIT THE LANDMARKS
(HEBREWS 11)

Journeys often include interesting and memorable landmarks. Perhaps you have visited Mount Rushmore, the Alamo, or the Statue of Liberty. Such places remind us of people and events that shaped our country and inspire us to good citizenship.

In Hebrews 11, the writer presented a list of human "landmarks"—special people in Jewish history. These Old Testament heroes and heroines set stirring examples of trust in God's promises. The registry, called "Faith's Hall of Fame," includes names, activities, sufferings, and blessings to encourage and strengthen Christians.

Description and Benefits of Faith (Hebrews 11:1-3)
1 *Now faith is the substance of things hoped for, the evidence of things not seen.* **2** *For by it the elders obtained a good testimony.* **3** *By faith we understand that the worlds were framed by the word of God, so that the things which are seen were not made of things which are visible.*

Faith is the assurance that sustains us on our Christian journey. Hebrews 11:1 gives a description: "Now faith is the substance of things hoped for, the evidence of things not seen." Faith is belief in God's promises. It is the staying power that helps us persevere. It provides proof for the eternal blessings not yet real for us.

Some deny that faith is rational. Yet everyone has faith in something. For instance, many are *certain* that if they earn a college degree, they will get a good job. They show faith by enrolling in courses. Being certain of something you cannot yet see is faith. Barmby wrote,

Even in ordinary affairs of life, and in science too, men act, and must act, to a great extent on faith; it is essential for success, and certainly for all great achievements—faith in the testimony and authority of others whom we can trust, faith in views and principles not yet veri-fied by our own experience, ... and so make ventures, on the ground, not of positive proof, but of more or less assured conviction. [158]

Our Christian faith is based on the testimony and authority of Scrip-ture. Hebrews readers revered their godly ancestors. So the writer pro-vided a gallery of ancients who believed God's word, received it, and acted on it. By faith each "obtained a good testimony [report]" from God (Hebrews 11:2).

Before listing names, the writer noted the readers' belief that God created the world (cf. Hebrews 11:3). We cannot empirically prove that our universe came into being by the word of an invisible power. We cannot comprehend this with the eye of reason. But we can with the eye of faith. Hebrews 11 names ancients who had absolute faith in God's promises. This list still encourages us today.

Pre-Flood Heroes (Hebrews 11:4-7)

4 *By faith Abel offered to God a more excellent sacrifice than Cain, through which he obtained witness that he was righteous, God testifying of his gifts; and through it he being dead still speaks.* **5** *By faith Enoch was taken away so that he did not see death, "and was not found, because God had taken him"; for before he was taken he had this testimony, that he pleased God.* **6** *But without faith it is impossible to please Him, for he who comes to God must believe that He is, and that He is a rewarder of those who diligently seek Him.* **7** *By faith Noah, being divinely warned of things not yet seen, moved with godly fear, prepared an ark for the saving of his household, by which he condemned the world and became heir of the righteousness which is according to faith.*

The writer first named three men who lived before the flood: Abel, Enoch, and Noah. Each was associated with good works and rewards.

Abel's sacrifice was recorded in Genesis 4:3-5. God accepted his animal sacrifice because he offered it by faith (Hebrews 11:4). Since faith comes by hearing the word of God (Romans 10:17), there had to be divine instruction concerning sacrifices. Abel obeyed by offering an animal; Cain did not. God called Abel a "righteous" man whose example still speaks.

Enoch walked with God (Genesis 5:21-24). This means they shared a close relationship. For his life of faith, Enoch was taken away without experiencing death. When Christ comes again, some will receive this same reward (1 Corinthians 15:52; 1 Thessalonians 4:17). Scripture testifies that Enoch pleased God (Hebrews 11:5). Verse 6 states the necessity of such faith: "But without faith it is impossible to please Him, for he who comes to God must believe that He is, and that He is a rewarder of those who diligently seek Him." God rewards those who please Him.

The third example, Noah, was known for building the ark (Genesis 6–8). He believed God's word concerning the unseen flood, and with reverential fear, he "did according to all that God commanded him" (Genesis 6:22; 7:5). For 120 years, he set an example before a wicked world. Milligan clarified, "He who gives heed to God's warnings and admonitions, condemns by his faith and practice all who neglect to do so."[159] So, as the world drowned, Noah and his family of eight souls were saved (1 Peter 3:20). God rewards faith and obedience (Hebrews 6:12).

How would you face life as the only believer
in your home, neighborhood, or workplace?

Abraham: Father of the Faithful (Hebrews 11:8-12)
8 *By faith Abraham obeyed when he was called to go out to the place which he would receive as an inheritance. And he went out, not knowing where he was going.* **9** *By faith he dwelt in the land of promise as in a foreign country, dwelling in tents with Isaac and Jacob, the heirs with him of the same promise;* **10** *for he waited for the city which has foundations, whose builder and maker is God.* **11** *By faith Sarah herself also received strength to conceive seed, and she bore a child when she was past the age, because she judged Him faithful who had promised.* **12** *Therefore from one man, and him as good as dead, were born as many as the stars of the sky in multitude—innumerable as the sand which is by the seashore.*

Abraham, the revered model of faith, "believed in the LORD, and He accounted it to him for righteousness" (Genesis 15:6). When God called, Abraham left the comforts of his home among the Chaldeans and lived as a foreigner in an unknown land (12:1-4).

Because of God's promise, Abraham believed his descendants would one day possess the land in which he lived. He also had faith that he and his spiritual descendants would inherit eternal life in the heavenly city (John 8:56). While in Canaan, Abraham's home was a temporary tent. He looked forward with the eye of faith to an eternal, permanent dwelling that God Himself would build. Lightfoot compared his lot with first-century readers:

> The experiences through which Abraham passed were remarkably like the circumstances of the original readers of the Epistle. Abraham had received a call to go forth, and they had been summoned to go forth to Jesus outside the camp, taking His stigma. Abraham had wandered about in Canaan, finding no certain home; they, too, as strangers and passing travelers on earth, had to look to the eternal city.[160]

Abraham's son and grandson, Isaac and Jacob, also lived as strangers in the Promised Land. They, too, had faith in future possession of that country. They also believed in a heavenly inheritance. And they were rewarded for their faith and perseverance.

Sarah, Abraham's wife, was one of only two women listed (cf. Hebrews 11:11). Yes, we know of her doubt. Perhaps it was because Sarah was *not* perfect and rose above her failures that she was included. Hebrews 11 does not mention her faults, only her circumstances. She was an example of faith, one of the "holy women" and the mother of spiritual daughters who follow her example (1 Peter 3:5-6). Sisters, is it not comforting to know that, despite our weaknesses, God can count us faithful?

Because of their faith, Abraham and Sarah, too old to have children, were rewarded by God with many descendants. Milligan stated, "Nothing could better serve to strengthen the hands and encourage the hearts of the desponding and persecuted Hebrews, than this reference to the faith of their illustrious ancestor."[161]

*Are you one of Sarah's "daughters"? Discuss her
faith in the move at God's call, her conception of Isaac,
and her traits as described in 1 Peter 3:5-6.*

Patient Patriarchs (Hebrews 11:13-16)

13 *These all died in faith, not having received the promises, but having
seen them afar off were assured of them, embraced them and confessed
that they were strangers and pilgrims on the earth.* **14** *For those who say
such things declare plainly that they seek a homeland.* **15** *And truly if they
had called to mind that country from which they had come out, they would
have had opportunity to return.* **16** *But now they desire a better, that is, a
heavenly country. Therefore God is not ashamed to be called their God, for
He has prepared a city for them.*

Abraham, Isaac, and Jacob lived in Canaan, but did not possess it.
They called themselves pilgrims in that land (Genesis 23:3-4; 24:37;
47:9). To them, the earthly Promised Land was a blessing for their descendants, but they themselves looked forward to the spiritual home
God had promised. Lenski noted, "They were like pilgrims to the Holy
City who see its towers and spires on the horizon, ecstatically point
to the vision and shout their acclaim. This is all they had during their
earthly lives."[162]

These faithful, tent-dwelling nomads sought not a permanent homeland, but an eternal one. They did as Christians are directed to do: they
set their affections on things above and not on things of the earth (Colossians 3:2). Lenski applied this to readers:

> As former Jews Abraham, Isaac, and Jacob are their great examples of
> faith. See these patriarchs disregard everything in the way of an earth-
> ly fatherland, pass through life and die as nothing but aliens among
> men, aliens in fact, yea, aliens because they are ever aspiring to a bet-
> ter, a heavenly fatherland, the City of God, prepared for them by God.
> Will the readers do less?[163]

God rewarded these faithful patriarchs, identifying Himself as
the God of Abraham, Isaac, and Jacob (Exodus 3:6, 15). Christ, too,

will stand up for us if we confess His name before others (Matthew 10:32-33). Those who demonstrate faith are rewarded.

What does the term "aliens" mean to
you in light of our spiritual destination?

Faith Tested and Shared (Hebrews 11:17-22)

17 *By faith Abraham, when he was tested, offered up Isaac, and he who had received the promises offered up his only begotten son,* **18** *of whom it was said, "In Isaac your seed shall be called,"* **19** *concluding that God was able to raise him up, even from the dead, from which he also received him in a figurative sense.* **20** *By faith Isaac blessed Jacob and Esau concerning things to come.* **21** *By faith Jacob, when he was dying, blessed each of the sons of Joseph, and worshiped, leaning on the top of his staff.* **22** *By faith Joseph, when he was dying, made mention of the departure of the children of Israel, and gave instructions concerning his bones.*

Readers were next reminded that God asked Abraham to offer his son, Isaac. This referred again to Abraham's test of faith to sacrifice his son (Genesis 22). As he thrust his hand downward with the knife, God stopped him, saying, "Do not lay your hand on the lad, or do anything to him; for now I know that you fear God, since you have not withheld your son, your only son, from Me" (v. 12). What was nearly done to Isaac (a type of Christ) was actually done by God with His own Son.[164]

Abraham had mentally given up Isaac for dead. He believed that God would fulfill His promise by resurrecting the boy (Genesis 22:5). In a figurative sense, he received him "from the dead" (Hebrews 11:19). God did not want Isaac's life; He wanted Abraham's heart. Later, God reiterated His covenant to Isaac and Jacob (Genesis 26:1-4; 28:10-14). Each believed and was rewarded. Their faith showed in the blessings they gave to their own sons. Isaac blessed Jacob and Esau through faith in unseen matters (27:26-29, 38-40). Jacob blessed Joseph's sons, Ephraim and Manasseh, with faith in God's promises for the future (48:14-20). Joseph asked that his bones be buried in the Promised Land when his descendants would possess it (49:29; 50:24-25; Joshua 24:32).

The Faith of Moses (Hebrews 11:23-28)

23 *By faith Moses, when he was born, was hidden three months by his parents, because they saw he was a beautiful child; and they were not afraid of the king's command.* **24** *By faith Moses, when he became of age, refused to be called the son of Pharaoh's daughter,* **25** *choosing rather to suffer affliction with the people of God than to enjoy the passing pleasures of sin,* **26** *esteeming the reproach of Christ greater riches than the treasures in Egypt; for he looked to the reward.* **27** *By faith he forsook Egypt, not fearing the wrath of the king; for he endured as seeing Him who is invisible.* **28** *By faith he kept the Passover and the sprinkling of blood, lest he who destroyed the firstborn should touch them.*

Moses, the great mediator of God's old covenant, was also on the list. His faith, influenced by his parents, was often noted. Moses was born in a sad time in Hebrew history. To prevent population growth, Pharaoh commanded all Hebrew, male babies to be thrown into the Nile River. But Moses' parents saw that he was "a beautiful child" and hid him three months. They trusted God for his preservation. Exodus 2 records his placement in a basket in the Nile and his adoption by Pharaoh's daughter. Moses' mother, Jochebed, was rewarded for her faith. She was allowed to nurse him and teach him about his true heritage. Exell wrote, "Hence he would go to the Egyptian court with a knowledge of his country's woe—and of his father's God."[165]

Raised in Pharaoh's house, Moses was instructed in all the wisdom of the Egyptians (Acts 7:22), but he held to his parents' faith. As an adult, he rejected the splendor of Egypt—its treasures, power, and privilege (the fleeting pleasures of sin)—and chose God's people (a nation of slaves) with their poverty, contempt, and affliction.[166] He accepted the kind of rejection and abuse that afflicted Christ and those who follow Him (2 Timothy 3:12). Moses believed the promise—not only that God's people would possess Canaan, but that he would someday enter into God's heavenly rest.

With an eye of faith, Moses represented the King of heaven by boldly demanding of Pharaoh, "Let My people go!" (Exodus 9:1). He pronounced the ten plagues and inaugurated the Hebrew Passover. For this memorial, he instructed the Israelites to sprinkle lamb's blood over their doorposts to protect their firstborn. This was all done by faith.

Discuss Jochebed's faith and God's providence in saving baby Moses.
Give examples from your own life of living in bold faith.

Faith Shown in the Exodus and at Jericho (Hebrews 11:29-31)
29 *By faith they passed through the Red Sea as by dry land, whereas the Egyptians, attempting to do so, were drowned.* **30** *By faith the walls of Jericho fell down after they were encircled for seven days.* **31** *By faith the harlot Rahab did not perish with those who did not believe, when she had received the spies with peace.*

The writer of Hebrews next revealed the influence of Moses' faith on the people of Israel. They demonstrated faith in God after their deliverance. Soon after leaving Egypt, they came to the Red Sea. With no boat and no bridge, they were frightened by Pharaoh's approaching army. They cried out, and Moses demonstrated faith in the unseen path to safety. He proclaimed, "Do not be afraid. Stand still, and see the salvation of the LORD, which He will accomplish for you today. For the Egyptians whom you see today, you shall see again no more forever" (Exodus 14:13). The children of Israel responded with faith (v. 31; Hebrews 11:29). It is sad that their faith was short-lived and that they did not enter the Promised Land. Yet in Hebrews doubt was not mentioned, only faith and its rewards.

Israel's second generation learned from the first and crossed the Jordan River into Canaan (Joshua 3). They marched around the walls of Jericho toward a victory seen only through faith (6:1-5; Hebrews 11:30). One woman, Rahab, was saved from the destruction because she shared the Israelites' faith (Joshua 2:1, 11; Hebrews 11:30-31). Rahab was named not only in Hebrews 11, but also in Jesus' genealogy (Matthew 1:5). Those who diligently seek God and believe are rewarded.

Moses inspired faith in Israel. Name a faithful
model in your life who has influenced you.

Other Examples of Faith (Hebrews 11:32-40)

32 *And what more shall I say? For the time would fail me to tell of Gideon and Barak and Samson and Jephthah, also of David and Samuel and the prophets:* **33** *who through faith subdued kingdoms, worked righteousness, obtained promises, stopped the mouths of lions,* **34** *quenched the violence of fire, escaped the edge of the sword, out of weakness were made strong, became valiant in battle, turned to flight the armies of the aliens.* **35** *Women received their dead raised to life again. Others were tortured, not accepting deliverance, that they might obtain a better resurrection.* **36** *Still others had trial of mockings and scourgings, yes, and of chains and imprisonment.* **37** *They were stoned, they were sawn in two, were tempted, were slain with the sword. They wandered about in sheepskins and goatskins, being destitute, afflicted, tormented—***38** *of whom the world was not worthy. They wandered in deserts and mountains, in dens and caves of the earth.* **39** *And all these, having obtained a good testimony through faith, did not receive the promise,* **40** *God having provided something better for us, that they should not be made perfect apart from us.*

So many examples exist that the writer could not have named them all. He listed six more heroes and then briefly mentioned other faithful activities and rewards.

We can read of the conquests of Gideon and Barak, the victories of Samson and Jephthah, and the leadership of King David, the judge/prophet Samuel, and the other prophets. These heroes were flawed but faithful. They believed in God and His rewards. Lenski called this "a gallery of notable portraits of ancient great believers, each drawn with a master hand. They all believed the unseen, they all trusted a promise, things for which they had to wait and hope. One grand characteristic makes them all kin—faith."[167]

Among the heroes and heroines named in Hebrews 11:4-32, whose life of faith inspires you the most? Why?

More were listed, though not by name but by achievements. The writer explained that they subdued kingdoms (Judges 11:32-33), worked righteousness (2 Samuel 8:15), obtained promises (Hebrews 6:13-15), stopped the mouths of lions (Daniel 6:22), quenched the violence of fire (3:27), escaped the edge of the sword (1 Kings 19:1-3), out of weakness were made strong (Judges 16:28), became valiant in battle (4:16), and turned to flight the armies of the aliens (7:22). God rewards faith.

Hebrews 11:35 states that women received their dead raised to life again. This included the widow of Zarephath and the Shunammite woman, whose sons were raised by Elijah and Elisha, respectively (1 Kings 17:17-24; 2 Kings 4:32-37).

Because readers needed encouragement in persecution, the writer listed sufferings endured by the faithful. These chose to accept torture rather than to miss their reward: the better resurrection (Hebrews 11:35). While many lived in Old Testament times, scholars include intertestamental incidences closer to the readers' lifetime. Second Maccabees' historical accounts reveal the tortures of a man named Eleazar and of a woman and her seven sons, who were mutilated, flayed, and roasted in fire (2 Maccabees 6:19-29; 7).[168]

Hebrews 11:36-37 lists mockings (2 Chronicles 36:16), scourgings, chains (Jeremiah 20:2), imprisonment (38:6), being stoned, being sawn in two (Isaiah, by tradition), and being tempted and slain with the sword (Jeremiah 26:23). These were endured by men and women who refused to deny their faith and who trusted in God's promise of a better life beyond the grave.

How is knowledge of Old Testament
accounts helpful in understanding Hebrews?

Some lived with rejection from a world unworthy of their godly example. Without homes and means of support, they wandered in animal skins, "destitute, afflicted, and tormented" (Hebrews 11:37). Milligan states that this closing remark is applicable to the Maccabean period, when "the mountains and caves of Judea were filled with pious sufferers."[169] Sisters, our trials pale in comparison with these godly sufferers who inspire us.

These models of faith lived before Christ. They are commended for their faith in God's promise of a new High Priest and a better covenant. Only by faith did they envision the hoped-for blessings (Hebrews 11:13). Lightfoot stated, "To them belonged the promise; to the saints of the new age belongs the fulfillment. It is in the new age that the better things are provided—the better covenant, with complete forgiveness of sins, the better hope, and so on."[170]

The last two verses of Hebrews 11 conclude, "And all these, having obtained a good testimony through faith, did not receive the promise, God having provided something better for us, that they should not be made perfect apart from us" (vv. 39-40). They were not cleansed apart from the Christianity we enjoy. The blood of Christ Jesus made them whole too. Lightfoot beautifully summarized,

> Thus the author has come again to the main thrust of the Epistle. It was because of faith that the men of old were attested to (v.2), a faith that surrendered all. This was the glory of Israel's heritage, from the blood of Abel to the martyrdom of the Maccabean zealots. Yet even so, this was but a preparation, a scheme of preliminary measures that find their true meanings only in Christ. In Him alone there is hope. Why, then, should the readers of the Epistle forsake their only way of salvation, the only One through whom could be obtained the promises the fathers never quite realized? The correct answer to this question, logically deduced from Biblical proofs, was to the author the surest antidote for apostasy.[171]

SUMMARY AND LOOKING FORWARD TO THE NEXT CHAPTER

This chapter focused on the importance of faith. The writer listed the names of faithful ancients with their good works and rewards. These included Noah, Abraham, Sarah, Moses, Rahab, and more. Many others suffered. They never received the promises on earth but were commended for their faith. In Hebrews 12, we will read about the spiritual place promised to Christians called Zion. It is a difficult journey, so the writer encouraged spiritual travelers to help the weak, pursue peace, and beware of ingratitude and defiance against God.

CHAPTER 12

HEAVEN IS THE BETTER PLACE
(HEBREWS 12)

As a child, did you have a favorite travel destination? My sisters and I enjoyed our annual family trips to Texas to visit grandparents. Of course, we wanted to go to Disneyland, but it was too far away. Another place of interest to me was Zion. I had no idea where it was, but I knew it must be a wonderful place. People at church were always singing about marching to Zion, the city of God.

We all want to go to heaven. It is the goal of our Christian journey. The writer of Hebrews stressed the fact that we can only enter that rest if we persevere to the end. Some have a short trip; others travel for years. But no one can sprint to heaven. The Christian journey is a marathon.

A Heavenly Race (Hebrews 12:1-3)
1 Therefore we also, since we are surrounded by so great a cloud of witnesses, let us lay aside every weight, and the sin which so easily ensnares us, and let us run with endurance the race that is set before us, 2 looking unto Jesus, the author and finisher of our faith, who for the joy that was set before Him endured the cross, despising the shame, and has sat down at the right hand of the throne of God. 3 For consider Him who endured such hostility from sinners against Himself, lest you become weary and discouraged in your souls.

Hebrews compares Christianity to an Olympic race. Just as athletes run around the stadium in hopes of winning the victory crown, Christians run their race toward a heavenly reward. And just as thousands of spectators cheer in the stadium, we have a great "cloud of witnesses" made up of faithful saints who have finished their course. Their examples encourage us to throw off sinful hindrances and run with perseverance.

The term "race" in Hebrews 12:1 means an "agonizing, grueling course that requires Christian endurance if one is to win."

The term "race" (*agona*) in Hebrews 12:1 means an "agonizing, grueling course that requires Christian endurance if one is to win."[172] But, as Old Testament models prove, the heavenly marathon can be run successfully. It requires two things: (1) We must get rid of every sin that hinders us, "like a trailing garment that threatens to entwine about a runner's feet,"[173] and (2) we must keep going until we cross the finish line. Only those who finish will receive a crown (1 Corinthians 9:24-25).

Paul testified that he finished the race, kept the faith, and anticipated a heavenly crown (2 Timothy 4:7-8). The heroes and heroines listed in Hebrews 11 are godly models. But there is one example on whom we must keep our eyes fixed: Jesus. He ran the race. He endured hostility and death. And He persevered to the end (cf. Hebrews 12:2-3). By keeping our eyes on Jesus, we can avoid distractions of the world that hinder us from reaching the goal. He is the pioneer who first led the way to heaven, and He is the finisher who brought salvation to its completion through His death.

In His earthly journey, Jesus endured two main difficulties: hostile enemies and the cross. Pure hearts loved Him, but the wicked hated and crucified Him. We cannot comprehend the pain and shame of the cross. In the first century, this wooden torture stick was not a cherished symbol hung on the wall or on one's neck. It represented the most painful and degrading death used only for the worst criminals (Galatians 3:13).

Jesus submitted to this suffering because it was God's plan for our redemption. He was able to persevere by focusing on the joy of His reward. His reward included exaltation by God, a name above every name, and a seat at the right hand of the throne (Philippians 2:9; Hebrews 1:3). His model of patient endurance can help us when we grow weary and discouraged. We must focus on Jesus and on our reward at the end.

What are some ways we can keep our
eyes on Jesus in this present life?

Appreciate Discipline (Hebrews 12:4-11)

4 *You have not yet resisted to bloodshed, striving against sin.* **5** *And you have forgotten the exhortation which speaks to you as to sons: "My son, do not despise the chastening of the LORD, nor be discouraged when you are rebuked by Him;* **6** *for whom the LORD loves He chastens, and scourges every son whom He receives."* **7** *If you endure chastening, God deals with you as with sons; for what son is there whom a father does not chasten?* **8** *But if you are without chastening, of which all have become partakers, then you are illegitimate and not sons.* **9** *Furthermore, we have had human fathers who corrected us, and we paid them respect. Shall we not much more readily be in subjection to the Father of spirits and live?* **10** *For they indeed for a few days chastened us as seemed best to them, but He for our profit, that we may be partakers of His holiness.* **11** *Now no chastening seems to be joyful for the present, but painful; nevertheless, afterward it yields the peaceable fruit of righteousness to those who have been trained by it.*

Obstacles in life exist, in part, because God allows them. They have a purpose. The author of Hebrews compared these to the discipline a loving father provides for his children. Readers thought they had it rough, but their hardships were minor compared to others who had been killed for their faith. The writer reminded them, "You have not yet resisted to bloodshed" (Hebrews 12:4). Paul proclaimed, "All who desire to live godly in Christ Jesus will suffer persecution" (2 Timothy 3:12). Did these Christians assume they were exempt? Do we?

When given by the Lord, trials are meant to be beneficial. The writer quoted Proverbs 3:11-12 (cf. Hebrews 12:5-6). When we view difficulties with the right perspective, we grow spiritually. James shared the practicality and wisdom of Proverbs by urging, "Count it all joy when you fall into various trials, knowing that the testing of your faith produces patience. But let patience have its perfect work, that you may be perfect and complete, lacking nothing" (James 1:2-4). Trials can increase spiritual maturity and the ability to persevere. They do not imply anger or abandonment by God. On the contrary, if we do not receive chastening, we are not His children. Trials given by the Lord are actually evidences of sonship, which the writer explained in Hebrews 12:7-11.

Did you have a loving father who cared enough to correct you when you did wrong? If so, you were blessed. You probably did not appreciate it at the time, but as adults, we love them for this training. So if we respect our earthly fathers, the writer asked, "Shall we not much more readily be in subjection to the Father of spirits and live?" (Hebrews 12:9). Human fathers are inconsistent and make mistakes in chastening. Did you ever receive punishment for something you did not do? But God is perfect. His love is perfect. His discipline is perfect. Seeing this with the right attitude will bring us peace, joy, and strength (Psalm 119:67, 71; Romans 5:3-4; 2 Corinthians 4:17).

Discuss your experience with discipline as a child
and how you feel about your earthly father now.

To reject God's good purposes will make us bitter and spiritually weak. One commentary stated that we cannot go to heaven without "passing through the furnace of afflictions" (Acts 14:22).[174] This reminded me of a story titled "The Refiner's Touch," which is about God's role as a refiner of silver (Malachi 3:3). A ladies Bible study group wanted to better understand this concept, so

> one of the women offered to find out about the process of refining silver and get back to the group at their next Bible study. That week the woman called up a silversmith and made an appointment to watch him at work. She didn't mention anything about the reason for her interest in silver beyond her curiosity about the process of refining silver. As she watched the silversmith, he held a piece of silver over the fire and let it heat up. He explained that, in refining silver, one needed to hold

the silver in the middle of the fire where the flames were hottest so as to burn away all the impurities.

The woman thought about God holding us in such a hot spot, and then she thought again about the verse, that He sits as a refiner and purifier of silver. She asked the silversmith if it was true that he had to sit there in front of the fire the whole time the silver was being refined. The man answered that yes, he not only had to sit there holding the silver, but he had to keep his eyes on the silver the entire time it was in the fire, for if the silver was left even a moment too long in the flames, it would be destroyed.

The woman was silent for a moment. Then she asked the silversmith, "How do you know when the silver is fully refined?" He smiled at her and answered, "Oh, that's the easy part—when I see my image reflected in it."[175]

This beautiful analogy can help us endure afflictions. Trials assure us that we are legitimate children of God. They help us partake of His holiness. They yield "the peaceable fruit of righteousness" (Hebrews 12:11). Discipline should not discourage us; it should motivate us to persevere. We must imitate the faithful, ancient heroes and heroines, keep our eyes on Jesus, and develop camaraderie among our spiritual brothers and sisters.

Have you or has someone you know endured a very difficult trial? If so, describe it and the outcome.

Encourage One Another (Hebrews 12:12-17)
12 *Therefore strengthen the hands which hang down, and the feeble knees,* **13** *and make straight paths for your feet, so that what is lame may not be dislocated, but rather be healed.* **14** *Pursue peace with all people, and holiness, without which no one will see the Lord:* **15** *looking carefully lest anyone fall short of the grace of God; lest any root of bitterness springing up cause trouble, and by this many become defiled;* **16** *lest there be any fornicator or profane person like Esau, who for one morsel of food sold his birthright.* **17** *For you know that afterward, when he wanted to inherit the blessing, he was rejected, for he found no place for repentance, though he sought it diligently with tears.*

Persecution and chastening occur in our heavenly journey; therefore, we need one another. Scripture compares the church to a body (1 Corinthians 12:12), with weak members described as having drooping hands, feeble knees, and lame feet (Hebrews 12:12-13). When parts of the body hurt, the whole body suffers; therefore, the Hebrews writer prompted readers to encourage one another.

The allusion to Isaiah 35:3 and Proverbs 4:26 in Hebrews 12:12-13 is a call for strong Christians to lift up the weak and remove obstacles from their way (Romans 15:1). If we do not, we may be pulled down. Lightfoot asserted, "Cowardice is contagious! Courage can revive sinking hearts and renew progress on the Christian way."[176] Yes, courage is essential to perseverance, but even more is required. We must engage in preventive maintenance to keep the weak from getting discouraged, falling away, and pulling others down.

A major preventive measure is to pursue peace and holiness (Hebrews 12:14). Of course, Christians are to seek peace with all men (Romans 12:18), but this is especially important within the church community. During times of persecution and other difficulties, it is easy to quarrel and divide. These actions discourage all—the weak and the strong—and they hurt the church's reputation in the community. Therefore, every member has the responsibility to pursue peace (showing forbearance and love) and holiness (living a life of service to God). A community of peaceful and holy members will look out for one another in their journey and will leave no one behind. Sisters, let us seek out and encourage the struggling women in our fellowship.

In congregations without peace and holiness, three progressive steps occur. Hebrews 12:14-17 explains: (1) discouraged members can lose God's grace for themselves, (2) they can contaminate others in the congregation, and (3) even if they later realize their sin, the damage can be irreparable.

First, discouraged members can turn from the Lord and lose His grace. It is imperative that we watch one another "carefully lest anyone fall short of the grace of God" (Hebrews 12:15). Yes, Christians can fall from grace. "Once saved, always saved" is a myth. Some can become weak and leave the faith because of neglect and lack of encouragement from the body. Pursuing peace means being patient with and loving the spiritually frail, drooping, and lame. Some specific actions include encouraging calls, emails, cards, and visits. We can also set an example of godliness and holy living. These activities strengthen the whole body. Failing to pursue peace and holiness has devastating effects.

Discuss actions we can take to prevent members
of our congregations from becoming discouraged.

Second, the fallen, disgruntled, and/or defiant members can contaminate others in the congregation. The old adage "hurt people hurt people" is true. An abundance of peace and holiness among members thwarts "any root of bitterness springing up" (Hebrews 12:15). This phrase refers to one who leaves the grace of God, becomes opposed to the faith, and causes trouble for others.

Third, damage to members and the church's reputation often cannot be undone. Hebrews 12:16-17 uses Esau as an example. He foolishly sold his birthright for a bowl of lentils (Genesis 25:29-34). The description of him as a "fornicator or profane person" implies a worldly mindset "in the sense of caring for nothing that is sacred or holy" because Esau treated his right of being firstborn as something secular or common in order to satisfy his appetite.[177]

Being one of God's children is a privilege. Trading it away for anything temporary is foolish. For one bowl of food, Esau gave away his rights to the family, property, and covenantal bloodline of the Messiah. The tragedy here is that "afterward, when he wanted to inherit the blessing, he was rejected, for he found no place for repentance, though he sought it diligently with tears" (Hebrews 12:17). Even if Esau repented, he could not get back what he lost. Sometimes the damage one inflicts on himself and others is irreparable. People who leave God's way and cause division can repent. But they often cannot undo the harm. If we are not careful, we can, by negligence and recklessness, forfeit our "birthrights as children of God."[178] The writer wanted readers to think, "Why would anyone settle for a mess of pottage when we have blessings in Christ and a heavenly destination?"

A Comparison of Sinai and Zion (Hebrews 12:18-24)
18 *For you have not come to the mountain that may be touched and that burned with fire, and to blackness and darkness and tempest,* **19** *and the sound of a trumpet and the voice of words, so that those who heard it begged that the word should not be spoken to them anymore.* **20** *(For they could not endure what was commanded: "And if so much as a beast touches the mountain, it shall be stoned or shot with an arrow."* **21** *And so terrifying was the sight that Moses said, "I am exceedingly afraid and trembling.")* **22** *But you have come to Mount Zion and to the city of the living God, the heavenly Jerusalem, to an innumerable company of angels,* **23** *to the general assembly and church of the firstborn who are registered in heaven, to God the Judge of all, to the spirits of just men made perfect,* **24** *to Jesus the Mediator of the new covenant, and to the blood of sprinkling that speaks better things than that of Abel.*

The goal of our Christian journey is heaven. We can reach it only through Christ and His church. But to some Hebrews readers, New Testament worship did not offer the awesome experience of coming before God in the Jewish temple. In Hebrews 12:18-24, the writer contrasted coming *before* God at the earthly Mount Sinai and coming *to* God in the spiritual realm of Zion.

When the Israelites came before God at Sinai, they gathered to hear the Old Law through Moses. It was an awesome experience, but in a terrifying way. It involved fire, darkness, a trumpet blast, death to any living thing that touched the mountain, and messages from God's voice that made the people tremble (Exodus 19:12-19; 20:18-19; Deuteronomy 5:22-25; 18:16; Acts 7:32). In Hebrews 12:18-20, the writer summarized these accounts. Read these Old Testament accounts to visualize the awesome, yet terrifying, experience for Israel.

Readers needed reminding that, at the covenant inauguration at Sinai, the people were afraid and unable to approach God. The ancient Israelites came before God, but they could not come to God. They had to stand afar off and fearfully experience His majesty and power.

But under the new covenant, God's people have full access to Him. We "have not come to the mountain [Sinai] that may be [physically] touched" (Hebrews 12:18). Sinai was not the final destination for God's people; it was a temporary "way station" for Israel, just as the Old Law.[180] God's plan is for all His people to come to a better place called Zion. It is the destination to which we travel until we gather with all God's people in eternal rest. What a contrast! Hebrews 12:22-24 describes this place.

Christians (spiritual Israel) enjoy a better experience. The writer exclaimed, "You have come to Mount Zion and to the city of the living God, the heavenly Jerusalem" (Hebrews 12:22). The verb "come" has the same root as the word for "a converted person (one who had turned)."[179] Pace confirmed, "Christians who had lived under the law had turned from that system and were to continue with Christ. In coming to Christ, they had been converted to all that the new covenant entailed. ... These brethren had already come to the holy city by entering into the church, the body of Christ."[181] Like them, we have been converted and come to Zion as members of the church, and we share spiritually in the city of the living God, the heavenly Jerusalem.

We have come to a better place! We sit in the heavenly places with Christ (Ephesians 2:6), and we look forward to entering the New Jerusalem, where God lives, at the end of our Christian journey (Psalm 9:11; Revelation 3:12; 21:2). The old Jerusalem, called Zion at its zenith, was a type of the heavenly city. God's presence was represented there in the ark of the covenant (2 Chronicles 5:2). Psalms, which foretold of the Messiah, includes references to this "holy hill of Zion" and the habitation of Jehovah (Psalm 2:6; 132:13).

Earthly Sinai was a type and shadow of the heavenly Zion. Sinai had no city; it was a mountain. Zion is not a mountain; it is a city, the city of the living God. It is a spiritual place where we live and serve Him until death transfers us to our final and permanent destination, heaven. There, innumerable angels stand around the throne of God (Revelation 5:11). There, we come to the "the heavenly counterpart to the earthly assembly" with the saved of all nations.[182] We come to the church of the firstborn—that is, the body of the One who ranks higher than all, even the hosts of heaven (Colossians 1:15). We come to the place where our names are written in the Book of Life (Luke 10:20; Philippians 3:20; 4:3).

The whole Zion experience is even more awesome than worship in the Jewish temple. Christians can approach God in prayer, and we will serve Him in the heavenly city (Revelation 22:3). We are in awe, but we do not tremble before the Judge, for we stand justified. Our spirits have been washed in the blood of the Lamb, and we have been made perfect (Hebrews 10:14). The word "perfect" here means "complete," and we are "brought to our final goal by blessed death" (Revelation 14:13).[183] Unlike the Israelites at Sinai, citizens of Zion will experience no more death, fear, fire, or darkness. All of the faithful will live forever in peace and comfort.

Compare Israel's experience at Sinai with our worship
to God. How do some today leave New Testament
worship to seek more "awesome" experiences?

Those making the Christian journey have a better path. As this letter states, we are on our way to the heavenly city, to thousands of angels, to God, and to the spirits of the saints. We have come to Jesus, the Mediator of this better covenant, and to the sprinkled blood that speaks a better word than the blood of Abel (Hebrews 12:24). When Abel was murdered, his blood cried out to God for vengeance (Genesis 4:10). But when our Mediator shed His blood on the cross, He cried out for pardon (Luke 23:34). The blood of Jesus ratified the covenant, and with that blood, our hearts are sprinkled (Hebrews 9:14; 10:22).

Listen to God and Be Grateful (Hebrews 12:25-29)
25 *See that you do not refuse Him who speaks. For if they did not escape who refused Him who spoke on earth, much more shall we not escape if we turn away from Him who speaks from heaven,* **26** *whose voice then shook the earth; but now He has promised, saying, "Yet once more I shake not only the earth, but also heaven."* **27** *Now this, "Yet once more," indicates the removal of those things that are being shaken, as of things that*

are made, that the things which cannot be shaken may remain. **28** *There-fore, since we are receiving a kingdom which cannot be shaken, let us have grace, by which we may serve God acceptably with reverence and godly fear.* **29** *For our God is a consuming fire.*

Our spiritual journey to Zion is filled with privileges better than those under the Law of Moses. Those who gathered at Sinai could only long for the coming of the Messiah, true forgiveness of sin, and a close relationship with God. He offered to bless them, and they agreed to follow Him. But they drifted, doubted, became dull of hearing, willfully sinned by refusing to listen to God's word, and lost their rest.

Up to this point, the Hebrews writer warned readers against four dangers. Now, he gave notice of one last soul-destroying act: defying the Word. It is the fifth and final warning. Those who despise and defy God's Word have fallen into full-blown apostasy.

- Do not *drift* from the Word—Hebrews 2:1-4 (neglect)
- Do not *doubt* the Word—Hebrews 3:7–4:13 (hard heart)
- Do not become *dull* toward the Word—Hebrews 5:11–6:20 (sluggishness)
- Do not *despise* the Word—Hebrews 10:26-39 (willfulness)
- **> Do not *defy* the Word—Hebrews 12:25-29 (refusing to hear)**

This warning begins with the same question asked in Hebrews 2:3. If those disobedient under the Law of Moses received severe penalties (Numbers 15:30), "How shall we escape if we neglect so great a salvation" as we enjoy in Christianity?

No one defies God without consequences. The children of Israel refused to keep their commitment and lost their relationship with God. They lost Canaan. They lost their eternal rest. How foolish for Christians to invite this fate by turning away from God's superior, gracious, and reassuring new covenant.

The Sinai experience reminds us of God's majesty and power. When He inaugurated the old covenant, the earth shook (Judges 5:4-5; Psalm 68:7-8). And God has promised a day in which He will once more "shake not only the earth, but also heaven"—that is, the celestial bodies that hang in the sky (Hebrews 12:26; cf. Haggai 2:6; Matthew 24:29). On that final day when Christ comes again, God will remove all transient "things that are made" in the physical sphere (Hebrews 12:27). This reminded readers that Mount Sinai, the Law of Moses, and Judaism were all temporary entities used by God for His purposes. The earth and its elements are also temporary creations used by God. After the mighty shaking, the only things left will be the permanent "things which cannot be shaken." This includes the heavenly kingdom, which we as Christians are in the process of receiving.

Jewish readers who desired the awesome experience of temple worship were reminded that God was still majestic and powerful. Therefore, the writer said, "Let us have grace, by which we may serve God acceptably with reverence and godly fear" (Hebrews 12:28). Our worship is to please Him, not ourselves. Service and gratitude please God and bring blessings. Defiance brings His wrath. Israel saw this part of His nature in the terrifying experience at Sinai. God has not changed. Hebrews 12:29 confirms, "Our God is a consuming fire."

How do we learn about service and worship that are acceptable to God? What is God's response to unacceptable acts?

SUMMARY AND LOOKING FORWARD TO THE NEXT CHAPTER

Hebrews 12 encourages Christians to run the Christian race to the end. We are encouraged by ancient heroes and heroines, Jesus, and our spiritual brothers and sisters. We are strengthened by God's discipline and trials by fire. This maturity is shown when we pursue peace, especially in the church, and unlike Esau, we must appreciate our spiritual privileges. The Hebrews writer explained that while those under the Law of Moses could come *before* God, Christians can come *to* God. He also gave the last of five warnings. We must listen to God's Word, be grateful, and persevere in the race to Zion. Chapter 13 contains the conclusion of the Hebrews letter.

CHAPTER 13

POSTSCRIPTS
(HEBREWS 13)

Here we are, near the end of this letter to the Hebrew Christians. And as some people add afterthoughts in postscripts (P.S.), this writer presented several short exhortations. He urged readers to continue in godly conduct (Hebrews 13:1-6), encouraged them to persevere in the Christian faith (vv. 7-17), made a personal plea (vv. 18-21), and ended with closing remarks (vv. 22-25).

Continue in Godly Conduct (Hebrews 13:1-6)
1 Let brotherly love continue. 2 Do not forget to entertain strangers, for by so doing some have unwittingly entertained angels. 3 Remember the prisoners as if chained with them—those who are mistreated—since you yourselves are in the body also. 4 Marriage is honorable among all, and the bed undefiled; but fornicators and adulterers God will judge. 5 Let your conduct be without covetousness; be content with such things as you have. For He Himself has said, "I will never leave you nor forsake you." 6 So we may boldly say: "The Lord is my helper; I will not fear. What can man do to me?"

The first exhortation is "let brotherly love continue" (Hebrews 13:1). The Greek word *philadelphia* refers to fraternal affection. These Christians were known for their works of love, such as their compassionate ministry toward the brethren (Hebrews 6:10; 10:32-33). This godly trait would bind them together in the midst of fear, persecution, and the temptation to leave Christianity. Detachment from one another was a danger for the readers, as it is for some today. Lenski wrote,

In our times, when so many false brotherhoods are established that claim to be superior to our brotherhood in Christ and urge their claims and their benefits to the detriment and even the disruption of our spiritual brotherhood in the faith and the confession of Christ, it is especially necessary to emphasize the divine character of the bond of brotherly love which unites us as believers in Christ and to urge all our brethren ever to continue therein and to cut loose from every antagonistic tie.[184]

Showing love was not new to Jews. In the Old Testament, God's people were instructed to help even strangers (Leviticus 19:34). But the "new" commandment given by Christ was a special, sacrificial love (John 13:34). This love was so evident among Christians that second-century historian Minucius Felix wrote, "They love one another almost before they know one another" (cf. v. 35).[185] Some assert that "kindness to strangers" was one reason for Christianity's rapid growth.[186] The writer reminded readers to continue showing kindness toward strangers and prisoners (Hebrews 13:2-3).

How does the "new" kind of love help Christians in times of persecution? How might we develop it in our hearts?

Christians must open their homes to people needing lodging and leave their homes to visit the imprisoned. In this, we do Christ's work on earth, as if helping Him (Matthew 25:38-40). The Old Testament reveals loving actions done unknowingly to angels (Genesis 18:2-10; 19:1-3, 15-16). In each, the one showing hospitality was blessed. Hebrews 13:2 suggests that when we show hospitality, we are blessed. Love and hospitality never go out of style, and in the first century, they were a physical necessity. Lightfoot clarified,

Especially among Christians, due to their particular circumstances, hospitality became a religious obligation. Christians often were on the road. Many were displaced and scattered from their native surroundings because of persecution; not a few went out preaching the gospel from place to place. The public inns were too costly for most Christians, and they were generally places of low repute. Special courtesies, then, were to be extended to all; "Practice hospitality ungrudgingly to one another" (1 Pet.4:9; cf. Rom.12:13).[187]

How can we follow the instruction to entertain strangers today?

The Hebrews readers lived in a time of Christian persecution. Some were imprisoned for their faith (Hebrews 10:34). Brethren were to visit, pray, and help with release, if possible. Any of us could end up in the same situation. Sisters, have you been mistreated for your faith? Did a Christian brother or sister show compassion for you?

In Hebrews 13:4, the subject shifts from purity in brotherly love to purity in the physical body. In that day, polygamy and concubines were tolerated by some Jews; and others, believing all sex was impure, practiced celibacy.[188] So the writer asserted, "Marriage is honorable among all, and the bed undefiled; but fornicators and adulterers God will judge." Physical intimacy is a God-given gift for married couples. But sexual immorality—as an unfaithful spouse (adultery) or as a willing participant in any sexual activity outside of marriage (fornication)—will be judged by God.

Another form of selfishness that will be judged is greed. Some had placed more confidence in worldly riches than in God. Hebrews 13:5 instructs, "Let your conduct be without covetousness; be content with such things as you have. For He Himself has said, 'I will never leave you nor forsake you'" (cf. Deuteronomy 31:6, 8; Joshua 1:5; 1 Chronicles 28:20). Christians whose homes had been robbed during persecution were suffering financial hardship. The writer encouraged them to keep the joyful spirit they had previously shown (Hebrews 10:34). Contentment was also emphasized in Luke 12:15-21 and 1 Timothy 6:7-10, 17-19.

The last postscript in this list was an exhortation to trust God to supply our needs and be with us through persecution. Hebrews 13:6 reads, "So we may boldly say: 'The LORD is my helper; I will not fear. What can man do to me?'" This quote, from Psalm 118:6, reminds the fearful to be confident in God's care (Matthew 6:25-33). Paul stated it another way: "If God is for us, who can be against us?" (Romans 8:31). These words provide strength today.

Why did the Jewish readers need these specific exhortations in Hebrews 13:1-6? Why do we need them today?

Persevere in the Christian Faith (Hebrews 13:7-17)
7 Remember those who rule over you, who have spoken the word of God to you, whose faith follow, considering the outcome of their conduct. 8 Jesus Christ is the same yesterday, today, and forever. 9 Do not be carried about with various and strange doctrines. For it is good that the heart be established by grace, not with foods which have not profited those who have been occupied with them. 10 We have an altar from which those who serve the tabernacle have no right to eat. 11 For the bodies of those animals, whose blood is brought into the sanctuary by the high priest for sin, are burned outside the camp. 12 Therefore Jesus also, that He might sanctify the people with His own blood, suffered outside the gate. 13 Therefore let us go forth to Him, outside the camp, bearing His reproach. 14 For here we have no continuing city, but we seek the one to come. 15 Therefore by Him let us continually offer the sacrifice of praise to God, that is, the fruit of our lips, giving thanks to His name. 16 But do not forget to do good and to share, for with such sacrifices God is well pleased. 17 Obey those who rule over you, and be submissive, for they watch out for your souls, as those who must give account. Let them do so with joy and not with grief, for that would be unprofitable for you.

The mentors and eyewitnesses of Christ who taught these readers were gone. The writer told them to draw encouragement from their memories (Hebrews 13:7). How blessed they were to have had examples who persevered in faith to the end and were worthy of imitation! Do you have such models of faith in your church family?

Of course, Jesus is the best example. He remains "the same yesterday, today, and forever" (Hebrews 13:8). Nothing about Him or His teachings has changed (Hebrews 1:12; James 1:17). His position as our great High Priest is unchangeable, as our faith should be. This concept would have helped readers reject the temptation to leave Christianity for Judaism or to be led away by any other "various and strange doctrines" (Hebrews 13:9; Ephesians 4:14). These truths still help us remain faithful.

Another issue facing the Hebrews readers was that certain teachers were trying to enforce Jewish restrictions of clean and unclean meats, but it was wrong to mix these rules with Christian doctrine. God's kingdom does not consist of meat and drink, but of grace, righteousness, peace, and joy in the Spirit (Hebrews 13:9; cf. Romans 14:17; 1 Corinthians 8:8). It is God's word and grace (undeserved favor) that establishes our hearts and helps us remain strong in the faith. It gives us stability, purpose, and consolation, and it makes us kind and benevolent like Christ.[189] Some Jews were proud of the fact that they were allowed to eat the sacrificial foods. However, that food was of no benefit. God's grace is the "food" that strengthens, and it is only enjoyed by Christians.

This privilege comes from Jesus' sacrifice. The Israelites and their priests ate at their altars (1 Corinthians 9:13; 10:18), but Christians "have an altar from which those who serve the tabernacle have no right to eat" (Hebrews 13:10). The Lord's sacrifice represents the altar we enjoy, and those who follow the Old Testament laws cannot participate in these blessings. Readers had to choose to remain in the church or lose these privileges by going back to temple worship.

Name some blessings we would lose if we left Christianity.

Of all the Jewish offerings, there was one of which no one ate. It was the high priest's sacrifice on the Day of Atonement. The remains of those animals were taken outside the camp and burned (Leviticus 6:30; 16:27). "Outside" the camp is significant because taking the slain animals away symbolized Israel's sin removal. It was also symbolic of Christ's sacrificial death "outside" Jerusalem, on Calvary, to sanctify the people. Hebrews 13:11-12 contrasts the old offerings (shadow) with the better sacrifice offered by our better High Priest.

Jesus' sacrifice differed from the deaths of animals in another aspect. He suffered. The cross was a death for criminals (Galatians 3:13).

It was agonizing and epitomized the rejection and suffering that we all, as sinners, would have had to endure. Those who left Judaism were similarly rejected and cast out by Jewish adherents. The writer exhorted readers to "make a clean break with unbelieving Israel"[190] and endure like Jesus (Hebrews 13:13). Following Christ involves rejection and suffering (2 Timothy 3:12).

Discuss the phrase "outside the gate" as used in Hebrews 13:12, and compare this with our treatment as Christians.

Christians with the right perspective can bear the reproach and persevere in the faith (1 Peter 4:14). This is the purpose of the Hebrews letter both for first-century converts and for us today. Lenski wrote,

> We have reached the climax of the epistle. From the start its aim has been to restore the wavering faith of the Jewish Christian readers in Jesus, to rid them of their recently conceived desire to go back to Judaism. To accomplish this effectively the break with their nation, with all Jews must be final, irrevocable, apparent at every turn. ... The writer includes himself; he adopts a wording from the ritual of Moses for the Day of Atonement, and he does this after the fullest preparation. Who could do better? We are Gentile Christians who are less apt to catch all the implications in the allusions; it will be well to work ourselves into them. We must read with Jewish eyes. The personal gain for us will be a better application to ourselves who must bear the world's reproach of Jesus and not merely the Jewish reproach.[191]

Staying focused on God's promised rest will help the rejected and outcast Christian. In Hebrews 13:14, readers were warned that Jerusalem, the city associated with Judaism, would soon fall. One writer called it "a temporary camp that will soon be broken up."[192] Similarly, Christians must disassociate from this world, which is not our home, and figuratively go outside the camp with Jesus. We look forward to the new, heavenly Jerusalem.

*As our world becomes more hostile toward Christianity,
how might the discussion in this chapter help us prepare?*

Jesus deserves our gratitude. We are saved because of His sacrifice, not dead animals. Readers needed to cling to this truth and let go of Levitical offerings. Christianity requires spiritual offerings of thanksgiving. Our words of praise are not mediated by earthly priests, but through our great High Priest (1 Peter 2:5). They are not offered annually, but continually. The Hebrews writer put it this way: "Therefore by Him let us continually offer the sacrifice of praise to God, that is, the fruit of our lips, giving thanks to His name" (Hebrews 13:15). Sisters, let us praise God in the name of Christ! Let us do it with thanksgiving!

With praise, we offer Christlike actions. Hebrews 13:16 states, "Do not forget to do good and to share, for with such sacrifices God is well pleased." We are to imitate Christ, who went about doing good. These Christians were urged to continue practicing love and care for one another. This is also a reminder for us today.

Because their former leaders and mentors were gone, readers were instructed to appreciate their present elders. God had given overseers the responsibility of watching over their souls (Acts 20:28; 1 Timothy 3:2; 1 Peter 5:1-4). Godly elders hold up the Christian faith and stop false teachers. The men overseeing these readers were duty-bound to warn the weak who were considering leaving Christianity.

In turn, members must receive the instruction of godly leaders (cf. Hebrews 13:17). Elders will answer to God for the way they lead, teach, and oversee. But it is difficult to lead if members will not follow. So we must make their job easy. Nothing gives elders more joy than to see members persevere in their journey toward heaven, and nothing saddens them more than to see some reject God's teachings and fall away. What is worse is the judgment on those who do not obey.

What should our attitude be toward our church elders?

A Personal Plea (Hebrews 13:18-21)

18 *Pray for us; for we are confident that we have a good conscience, in all things desiring to live honorably.* **19** *But I especially urge you to do this, that I may be restored to you the sooner.* **20** *Now may the God of peace who brought up our Lord Jesus from the dead, that great Shepherd of the sheep, through the blood of the everlasting covenant,* **21** *make you complete in every good work to do His will, working in you what is well pleasing in His sight, through Jesus Christ, to whom be glory forever and ever. Amen.*

The writer knew his readers and had even been with them for a time. Perhaps, while he was away, he heard this sermon and was concerned enough to write. In Hebrews 13:18-19, he requested prayers that he might be able to return. We all need prayers, especially elders, preachers, and missionaries. The writer and his companions expressed this need and shared feelings about the letter. It was not easy to write, especially the rebuke. But it was done with love and concern for their souls. If readers heeded, all would benefit.

The end of Hebrews sounds more like a letter. It follows the general form of Greek letters by including a prayer, final remarks, and greetings. Hebrews 13:20-21 presents the prayer. This congregation was in danger of division and apostasy.

The writer's prayer was that the God of peace, who raised Jesus and established the new covenant, would supply (make complete) their ability to serve Him. It also included a plea that He would be glorified forever. This section shows the writer's obvious love and concern for them.

How does it make you feel to hear that someone is praying for you?

Concluding Remarks (Hebrews 13:22-25)

22 *And I appeal to you, brethren, bear with the word of exhortation, for I have written to you in few words.* **23** *Know that our brother Timothy has been set free, with whom I shall see you if he comes shortly.* **24** *Greet all those who rule over you, and all the saints. Those from Italy greet you.* **25** *Grace be with you all. Amen.*

The writer made one final plea. He asked these brethren to read his message with kindness and patience. He reminded them why this was necessary. Their situation was critical; they needed a "word of exhortation" (Hebrews 13:22). He could have written more, but he tried to make it short. He begged their understanding because he cared about their feelings.

In Hebrews 13:23, he shared good news about Timothy's release. Lenski, who believes Apollos wrote the letter, stated, "It seems entirely natural to find him [Apollos] waiting for Timothy in order to return to Rome with him."[193] On the other hand, some assert that this verse harmonizes with a Pauline authorship because of his close relationship with Timothy.[194]

Because New Testament epistles rarely include an appeal to greet the leaders, Lightfoot suggested, "This might be an indication that the author is directing his letter to a smaller group within a larger one—either to a small group that was part of a church in a large city, or possibly to a small factious group that had withdrawn from the larger local church."[195] The salutation to "all the saints" is common in other letters (cf. Romans 1:7).

Hebrews 13:24 includes the line "Those from Italy greet you." Some suggest the writer was in Italy when he wrote this letter. Others say the readers were in Rome, while brethren from Italy were with the writer.

Hebrews ends with the conclusion we see in Paul's epistles: "Grace be with you all. Amen" (13:25; cf. Romans 16:24; Ephesians 6:24; Titus 3:15). Grace here implies "the special and peculiar favor of God to his children."[196]

This is a gift to all who follow Christ. To leave Christianity means giving up this favor and losing the eternal rest. Therefore, the writer ended with his wish for readers to remain faithful to the end.

"Grace" in Hebrews 13:25 implies "the special and peculiar favor of God to his children."

> *How does the Hebrews letter encourage*
> *you to persevere in the Christian faith?*

SUMMARY OF THE LETTER

Hebrews is an inspired letter written to struggling Jewish converts. Their lack of Bible study and fellowship had weakened them to the point that they could not handle the growing persecution. They were tempted to leave Christianity and return to the old Jewish system. Spiritually, they were drifting, doubting, dull of hearing, and in danger of full-blown apostasy through despising and defying God's Word. Their previous fervor and works of love needed rekindling.

The writer offered this brief word of encouragement. He reminded readers that Jesus is the better High Priest, who offered Himself as the better sacrifice and aids us in life as the better Mediator between God and His children. Jesus came to earth, lived as a human, and prepared our path to heaven. He is the author and finisher of our faith through whom God has promised eternal rest in heaven. Knowing these unchanging truths, readers then and today should be uplifted and motivated to persevere to the end. We do not walk alone. Our brethren and our Lord are with us on our journey to the better place!

NOTES

1. Neil R. Lightfoot, *Jesus Christ Today: A Commentary on the Book of Hebrews* (Grand Rapids: Baker, 1976) 31.

2. All quotes are from the New King James Version unless otherwise noted.

3. Walter Bauer, et al., *A Greek-English Lexicon of the New Testament and Other Early Christian Literature*, 2nd ed. (Chicago: University of Chicago Press, 1979) 449.

4. R.C.H. Lenski asserted that Apollos wrote Hebrews, probably in A.D. 68 or 69, after Paul's death. He used Acts 18:24-28; 1 Corinthians 16:10-12; and Titus 3:12-13 as evidence. See Lenski, *The Interpretation of the Epistle to the Hebrews and the Epistle of James* (Minneapolis: Augsburg Publishing House, 1966) 22-23.

5. Eusebius Ecclesiastical History 6.25.14. Qtd. in Leon Morris, *Hebrews (The Expositor's Bible Commentary)*, ed. Frank E. Gaebelein, vol. 12 (Grand Rapids: Zondervan, 1981) 7.

6. Lightfoot 31.

7. James Thompson, *The Letter to the Hebrews (The Living Word Commentary)* (Austin: R.B. Sweet, 1971) 8-9.

8. H.D.M. Spence and Joseph S. Exell, eds., *The Pulpit Commentary: Hebrews*, reprint, vol. 21 (Grand Rapids: Eerdmans, 1980) xvii.

9. Robert Milligan, *A Commentary on the Epistle to the Hebrews* (Nashville: Gospel Advocate, 1989) 26, 29.

10. Lenski suggested that the Palestinian persecution occurred before A.D. 35 and that those there who were not killed fled the country (363).

11. Ibid. 14-15.

12. Martel Pace, *Hebrews (Truth for Today Commentary)* (Searcy: Resource Publications, 2007) 15.

13. Spence and Exell xx.

14. Thompson 25.

15. Lightfoot 57.

16. In the New Testament world, one's name was important, for it "sums up all that a person is. One's whole character was implied in the name." See Leon Morris, *Hebrews (The Expositor's Bible Commentary)*, ed. Frank E. Gaebelein, vol. 12 (Grand Rapids: Zondervan, 1981) 16.

17. Lightfoot 58.

18. Spence and Exell 44.

19. Robert Tuck, "Hebrews," *The Preacher's Complete Homiletic Commentary*, reprint (Grand Rapids: Baker, 1980) 147.

20. Qtd. in David J. Riggs, "Are You Drifting?", http://oakridgechurch.com/riggs/drifting.htm, accessed 26 Jan. 2016. Happily, the author notes that he had baptized one of the men the week before.

21. Pace 73.

22. Lightfoot 70.

23. The Hebrews writer excluded himself from "those who heard" the gospel message firsthand. Theodore H. Robinson used this to eliminate Paul as the author, asserting that this statement "stands in strong contrast to the attitude of St. Paul, who, though not one of the original Twelve, yet always claimed that his authority was as direct and valid as theirs." See Robinson, *The Epistle to the Hebrews* (New York: Harper and Brothers, 1933) 13-14.

24. These are adapted from Warren W. Wiersbe, *The Bible Exposition Commentary: Ephesians–Revelation*, vol. 2 (Wheaton: Victor Books, 1989) 227.

25. "Incarnation," *Merriam-Webster.com*, Merriam-Webster, accessed 11 Nov. 2016.

26. Morris 27.

27. Ibid. 26.

28. "Son of man" is one way the ancients referred to man. Old Testament Hebrew poetry, as used in the psalms, often repeated a word or phrase in a different way, called synonymous parallelism.

29. Lightfoot 74.

30. Morris 25.

31. Ibid. 26.

32. Pace 87.

33. Thompson 45.

34. Morris 29.

35. Brett R. Scott, "Jesus' Superiority over Moses in Hebrews 3:1-6" *Bibliotheca Sacra* 155 (April–June 1996): 206.

36. Lightfoot 86.

37. Wiersbe 286-287.

38. Ibid. 287.

39. Thompson 57.

40. Lightfoot 90.

41. Bauer 617.

42. Pace 123.

43. Bauer 85.

44. "Journey," *Merriam-Webster.com*, Merriam-Webster, accessed 11 Nov. 2016.

45. Lenski 128.

46. Ibid. 133-134.

47. Lenski 133.

48. Lightfoot 97.

49. Thompson 64.

50. Bauer 763.

51. Pace 152.

52. James Thompson, "Striving for the Rest," *Truth for Today*, vol. 12 (June 1991) 18.

53. Ibid. 19.

54. Lenski 142, 144.

55. James Barmby, *The Pulpit Commentary: Hebrews*, eds. H.D.M. Spence and Joseph S. Exell, reprint, vol. 21 (Grand Rapids: Eerdmans, 1980) 111.

56. Lenski 142.

57. Thomas Hewitt, *The Epistle to the Hebrews: An Introduction and Commentary* (Grand Rapids: Eerdmans, 1960) 90.

58. Lightfoot 99.

59. Thompson, "Striving," 22.

60. Lightfoot 102.

61. Ibid. 101.

62. Ibid.

63. James Burton Coffman, *Commentary on Hebrews* (Austin: Firm Foundation, 1971) 97-98.

64. The New Open Bible, New King James Version, Study Edition (Nashville: Thomas Nelson, 1990) 1447.

65. Josephus, *Antiquities*, 15.3.1.

66. Russ Dudrey, "Gethsemane: The Fork in the Road (The Real Humanity of Jesus)" *Harvard Theological Review* 88 (January 1995): 167.

67. Pace 192. Lightfoot offered several ways that God may have answered Christ's prayer for deliverance, including easing His fear, sparing Him from premature death in the garden, and delivering Him from death by means of resurrection. See 109, 114-115.

68. Pace 208.

69. William Barclay, *The Gospel of Matthew*, vol. 2 (Philadelphia: Westminster Press, 1958) 385.

70. Martel Pace, "Indications of Immaturity: Hebrews 5:11-14." *Truth for Today* 26 (2006): 23.

71. Scot McKnight, "The Warning Passages of Hebrews: A Formal Analysis and Theological Conclusions." *Trinity Journal* 13 (1992): 44.

72. Leon Morris and Donald W. Burdick, *The Expositor's Bible Commentary: Hebrews, James* (Grand Rapids: Zondervan, 1996) 52.

73. Thomas G. Long, *Interpretation: Hebrews* (Louisville: Knox, 1997) 70.

74. W. Jones, *The Pulpit Commentary: Hebrews*, eds. H.D.M. Spence and Joseph S. Exell, reprint, vol. 21 (Grand Rapids: Eerdmans, 1980) 148.

75. "Titus Chapter 2." Bible-studys. org, accessed 11 Nov. 2016, http://www.bible-studys.org/ Bible%20Books/Titus/Titus%20 Chapter%202.html.

76. Thompson, "Striving," 24.

77. W.E. Vine, *Vine's Expository Dictionary of Old and New Testament Words*, vol. 2 (Old Tappen: Fleming H. Revell, 1981) 59.

78. Long 72.

79. Thompson, *The Letter*, 82-83.

80. Donald Guthrie, *The Letter to the Hebrews: An Introduction and Commentary* (Grand Rapids: Eerdmans, 1983) 137.

81. Gerhard Kittel and Gerhard Friedrich, eds. *Theological Dictionary of the New Testament*, vol. 1, (Grand Rapids: Eerdmans, 1984) 545.

82. Pace 219.

83. Lightfoot 126.

84. Lenski 186-187.

85. Morris and Burdick 55.

86. Bauer 184.

87. Pace, *Hebrews*, 234.

88. Thompson, "Striving," 27-28.

89. Lightfoot 130.

90. "Immutable," *Merriam-Webster. com*, Merriam-Webster, accessed 11 Nov. 2016.

91. Lenski 203.

92. Morris and Burdick 61.

93. Milligan 242-245.

94. Lenski 208.

95. Thompson, *The Letter*, 95.

96. For example, Jacob pronounced blessings upon his 12 sons (Genesis 49:28).

97. Pace, *Hebrews*, 263.

98. Thompson, "Striving," 99; Coffman 138-139.

99. Coffman 139.

100. Morris and Burdick 65.

101. Lightfoot 141.

102. Lenski 224; Lightfoot 143.

103. To "set aside" was a technical term used in legal documents meaning "to declare as void." See Lightfoot 143.

104. Lenski 231.

105. Milligan 267.

106. Lightfoot 145.

107. Josephus, *Antiquities*, 20.10.1. Qtd. in Lightfoot 145-146.

108. Milligan 270.

109. Lenski 242.

110. Pace, *Hebrews*, 242.

111. Roger L. Omanson, "A Superior Covenant: Hebrews 8:1–10:18," *Review & Expositor* 82.3 (Summer 1985): 361-362.

112. Milligan 301.

113. Pace, *Hebrews*, 299.

114. Morris and Burdick 75. Thompson also points out that the writer lived in a world permeated by Hellenistic thought and used rich Greek philosophical vocabulary: copy, shadow, pattern. He brought out the Greek idea of two realities: everything in the material world is but a "copy" of something that exists in the unseen world of ideas. See *The Letter* 111.

115. Pace, *Hebrews*, 299. Milligan added, "The sanctuary is heaven itself ... the archetype of the Most Holy Place of the ancient Tabernacle." See 276.

116. Milligan 278; Pace, *Hebrews*, 300.

117. Lightfoot 160-161.

118. Lightfoot 157.

119. Bauer 183.

120. Lenski 258-259.

121. Milligan 290.

122. Lightfoot 158-159.

123. Ibid. 157.

124. Pace, *Hebrews*, 307.

125. Thompson, "Striving," 31.

126. Lenski 269.

127. Lenski 302.

128. Milligan 309.

129. Several commentaries suggest that the golden censer was the altar of incense, which was required of the high priest before he entered (Exodus 40:5). Delitzsch says it was "not actually inside it," but belonged to the Holy of Holies "as the sign-board of a shop." Qtd. in Charles Jerdan, *The Pulpit Commentary: Hebrews*, eds. H.D.M. Spence and Joseph S. Exell, reprint, vol. 21 (Grand Rapids: Eerdmans, 1980) 227.

130. These examples come from Pace, *Hebrews*, 300 and Milligan 311.

131. Lenski 279.

132. Pace, Hebrews, 332.

133. F.F. Bruce, *The Epistle to the Hebrews (The New International Commentary on the New Testament)* (Grand Rapids: Eerdmans, 1964) 196.

134. Lightfoot 168.

135. Pace, *Hebrews*, 335.

136. Milligan 319.

137. Lightfoot 171.

138. Milligan 324.

139. Pace, *Hebrews*, 341.

140. Ibid. 351.

141. Lenski 293.

142. Milligan 325.

143. Bruce 219.

144. Bauer 92.

145. Pace, *Hebrews*, 354.

146. Ibid. 340.

147. Lightfoot 185.

148. Ibid. 187.

149. Lenski 351.

150. Bauer 629.

151. Lightfoot 191.

152. Milligan 366.

153. Lightfoot 107.

154. Ibid. 195.

155. Lenski 362.

156. Ibid. 366.

157. Ibid. 373.

158. Qtd. in Jerdan 297.

159. Milligan 394.

160. Lightfoot 209.

161. Milligan 399.

162. Lenski 396.

163. Ibid. 400.

164. Ibid. 404.

165. Joseph S. Exell, *The Preacher's Complete Homiletic Commentary on the Second Book of Moses Called Exodus* (Grand Rapids: Baker, n.d.) 16.

166. Lightfoot 215-216.

167. Lenski 372.

168. Ibid. 416-417.

169. Milligan 427.

170. Lightfoot 221-222.

171. Ibid. 222.

172. Coffman 286.

173. Lightfoot 228.

174. Milligan 449.

175. "The Refiner's Touch," accessed 12 Nov. 2016, http://www.clarion-call.org/extras/malachi.htm.

176. Lightfoot 234.

177. Lenski 447.

178. Milligan 461

179. Lenski 454.

180. Pace, *Hebrews*, 531.

181. Ibid.

182. Thompson, *The Letter*, 172.

183 Lenski 458.

184. Ibid. 468-469.

185. "New Advent," *Ante-Nicene Fathers*, trans. Robert Ernest Wallis, eds. Alexander Roberts, James Donaldson, and A. Cleveland Coxe, vol. 4 (Buffalo: Christian Literature, 1885). Revised and edited for New Advent by Kevin Knight, accessed 12 Nov. 2016, http://www.newadvent.org/fathers/0410.htm.

186. Milligan 481.

187. Lightfoot 246.

188. Lenski 471.

189. Milligan 488.

190. Lightfoot 252.

191. Lenski 486.

192. Milligan 491.

193. Lenski 498.

194. Milligan 500.

195. Lightfoot 256.

196. Milligan 501.

CPSIA information can be obtained
at www.ICGtesting.com
Printed in the USA
LVHW04s1006140918
589970LV00003B/4/P

9 780892 256693